Use YOUR Yardage!

13 Stash-Busting Quilts from Top Designers

C&T PUBLISHING

Publisher: Amy Marson

Creative Director: Gailen Runge

Project Editor: Alice Mace Nakanishi

Compiler: Lindsay Conner

Developmental Editors: Liz Aneloski, Cynthia Bix, Phyllis Elving, Lynn Koolish, Deb Rowden

Technical Editors: Carolyn Aune, Mary E. Flynn, Helen Frost, Doreen Hazel, Susan Nelsen, Sandy Peterson, Priscilla Read, Gailen Runge, Teresa Stroin, Janice Wray, Sadhana Wray, Nanette S. Zeller

Cover/Book Designer: April Mostek

Production Coordinators: Tim Manibusan and Zinnia Heinzmann

Illustrators: Mary E. Flynn, Jessica Jenkins, Tim Manibusan, Wendy Mathson, Amanda Murphy, Kirstie L. Pettersen, Aliza Shalit, Rose Sheifer, Amy Walsh, Janice Wray

Photography by Diane Pedersen, Christina Carty-Francis, and Nissa Brehmer, of C&T Publishing, Inc., unless otherwise noted

Published by C&T Publishing, Inc., P.O. Box 1456, Lafayette, CA 94549

Library of Congress Cataloging-in-Publication Data

Names: C & T Publishing, editor.

Title: Use your yardage! : 13 stash-busting quilts from top designers.

Description: Lafayette, CA : C&T Publishing, Inc., [2016] | Quilting by Alethea Ballard and others.

Identifiers: LCCN 2016025933 | ISBN 9781617454929 (soft cover)

Subjects: LCSH: Patchwork quilts. | Patchwork--Patterns.

Classification: LCC TT835 .U78 2016 | DDC 746.46--dc23

LC record available at https://lccn.loc.gov/2016025933

Printed in China

10 9 8 7 6 5 4 3 2 1

Contents

Basket Case

FINISHED QUILT: 65½″ × 81¾″

Designer: Angela Walters
Pieced by Mary Workman and Jessica Harrison; machine quilted by Angela Walters

When I set out to design a project that would showcase texture, all I could think about was a quilt that incorporated a weave element. After many tries, I finally came up with *Basket Case,* not your typical woven-looking quilt. With plenty of background area to showcase your favorite quilting design, this quilt will have people wanting to run their hands over it!

Materials

Cream solid: 5 yards with at least 42″ usable width for background

Blue solids: 2 shades totaling 2⅛ yards for blocks and binding

Batting: 74″ × 90″

Backing: 5⅛ yards

Cutting

Cream solid

- Cut 14 strips 1¼″ × width of fabric.
- Cut 13 strips 3¾″ × width of fabric; subcut as follows:

  For 8″ columns:

  30 segments 1¾″ × 3¾″

  32 segments 2½″ × 3¾″

  26 segments 3¼″ × 3¾″

  For 11″ columns:

  20 segments 1¾″ × 3¾″

  20 segments 3″ × 3¾″

  20 segments 3¾″ × 3¾″

  16 segments 4½″ × 3¾″

TIP *Cutting multiple strips at once will make the process go much more quickly.*

- Cut 2 strips 8″ × length of fabric (after you have cut the above strips); subcut into:

  8″ × 5½″ (Column 1a)

  8″ × 34½″ (Column 1b)

  8″ × 59″ (Column 2)

  8″ × 15¾″ (Column 5a)

  8″ × 11¼″ (Column 5b)

  8″ × 5¼″ (Column 8a)

  8″ × 31½″ (Column 8b)

- Cut 1 strip 4″ × 81¾″ (Column 6; cut lengthwise).
- Cut 2 strips 11″ × length of fabric; subcut into:

  11″ × 13¾″ (Row 3a)

  11″ × 39¼″ (Row 3b)

  11″ × 34¾″ (Row 7a)

  11″ × 18¼″ (Row 7b)

Blue solids

- Cut 14 strips 3″ × width of fabric.
- Cut 8 strips 2¼″ × width of fabric for binding.

Making the Quilt

1. Sew a cream strip 1¼″ × width of fabric to a blue strip. Press carefully. Repeat with the remaining 1¼″ cream strips and the remaining blue strips to make a total of 14 strip units.

2. Subcut the strips as follows:

For the 8″ column:	*For the 11″ column:*
7 strips, 8″ long	5 strips, 11″ long
15 strips, 5½″ long	10 strips, 8½″ long
16 strips, 4″ long	10 strips, 6″ long
13 strips, 2½″ long	10 strips, 4½″ long
	8 strips, 3″ long

3. Sew each size of blue-and-cream strip to the appropriate cream side pieces as shown in the diagrams below.

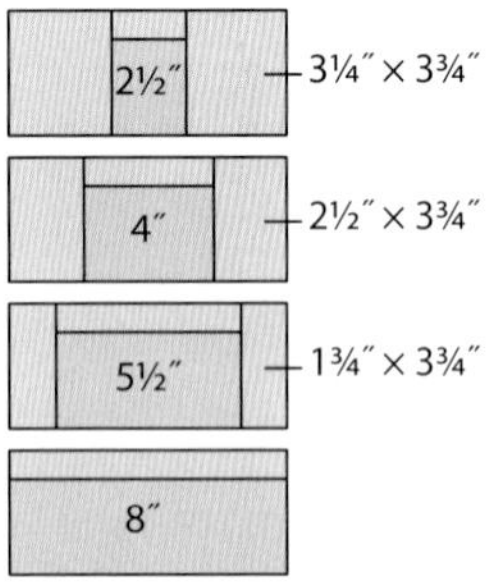

8″ block assembly

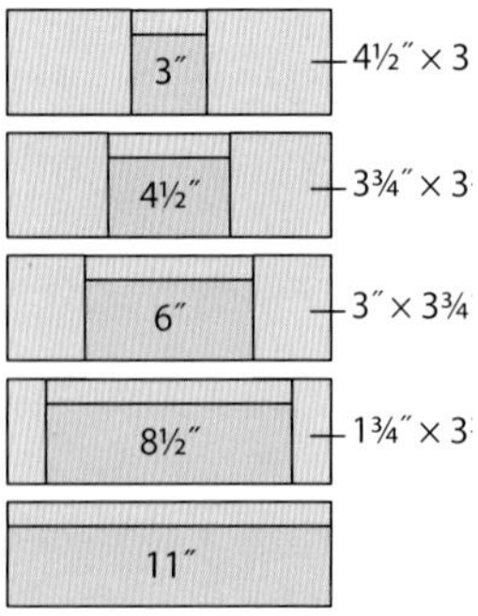

11″ block assembly

4. Piece the columns as shown in the quilt assembly diagram. Then sew the columns together in the indicated order to finish the quilt top.

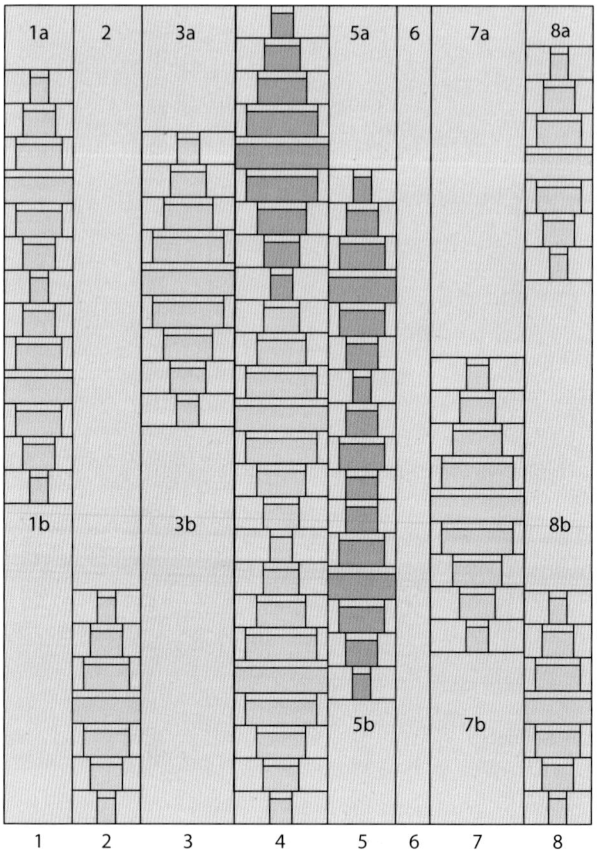

Quilt assembly

The Quilting

Layer the top, batting, and backing. Bind the quilt.

The choice of solid fabric for this quilt was not an accident! I wanted to be sure that the texture that quilting adds could be seen.

Crossroads

FINISHED QUILT: 65″ × 90″ ◆ **FINISHED BLOCK:** 8″ × 8″

Designer: Amanda Murphy

Pieced by Amanda Murphy; quilted by Deborah Norris

Fabrics: Blue and Aqua collection by Michael Miller Fabrics

Dynamic sashing strips and Checkerboard blocks enhance your favorite feature fabrics in this modern design. Choose sashing fabrics that read as solids to really make the blocks pop!

Materials

Light sashing and checkerboard fabric: 2¾ yards

Dark sashing, checkerboard, and inner border fabric: 2¼ yards

Feature fabrics: 31 squares 8½″ × 8½″

Inner border fabric: ½ yard

Outer border and binding fabric: 2 yards

Lightweight fusible interfacing: ¾ yard

Backing: 5¾ yards

Batting: 73″ × 98″ (such as Warm & Natural by The Warm Company)

Cutting

WOF = width of fabric

Light sashing and checkerboard fabric

- Cut 56 strips 1½″ × WOF.

Dark sashing and checkerboard fabric

- Cut 52 strips 1½″ × WOF. Set 8 of these strips aside for inner border.

Outer border and binding fabric

- Cut 9 strips 4¼″ × WOF for outer border.
- Cut 9 strips 2¼″ × WOF for binding.

Lightweight fusible interfacing

- Cut 14 strips 1½″ × WOF.

Block Assembly

1. Join 3 light sashing strips to 2 dark sashing strips, pressing seams toward the dark strips. Repeat to make 16 strip sets. Subcut strip sets into 60 units 8½″ wide and 64 units 1½″ wide.

2. Join 3 dark sashing strips 1½″ × WOF to 2 light sashing strips, pressing seams toward the dark strips. Repeat to make 4 strip sets. Subcut strip sets into 96 units 1½″ wide.

3. Join 2 units 1½″ wide from Step 1 and 3 units 1½″ wide from Step 2 together to make a checkerboard square. Repeat to make 32 checkerboard blocks. Press seams toward rows 1, 3, and 5.

Quilt Assembly

1. Following quilt assembly diagram 1, lay out the checkerboard, sashing, and feature fabric blocks to form the center of the quilt.

Quilt assembly 1

2. Join blocks into rows, pressing seams toward square units. Make sure that the raw edge of the short row extends ¼″ beyond the seam of the longer row. Press all seams toward square units.

3. Join rows.

4. Trim the quilt center down to size by cutting ¼″ out from the corner points of the blocks, as shown. The dotted line indicates the seamline—*not* the cutting line! Cut ¼″ out from dotted line.

5. Turn the quilt top over. Being careful not to stretch the edges of the quilt, apply interfacing along the perimeter, flush with the quilt top's edge. This will stabilize the bias edges that are exposed before adding borders.

6. The center of my quilt top after trimming was 55½″ × 80½″. Measure yours and adjust the following border measurements accordingly.

7. Piece 2 inner border strips 1½″ × 80½″ and sew onto each side of the quilt top. Piece 2 inner border strips 1½″ × 57½″ and sew onto the top and bottom of the quilt top.

8. Piece 2 outer border strips 4¼″ × 82½″ and sew onto each side of the quilt top. Piece 2 outer border strips 4¼″ × 65″ and sew onto the top and bottom of the quilt top.

Quilt assembly 2

Finishing

1. Divide backing fabric into 2 lengths. Cut 1 piece lengthwise to make 2 narrow panels. Join 1 narrow panel to each side of the wide panel. Press seams open.

2. Layer backing, batting, and quilt top. Quilt as desired.

3. Join the 2¼″-wide binding strips into 1 continuous piece for the binding. Press, folding in half lengthwise. Sew the binding to the quilt. Enjoy!

STEPHANIE KAZA
THE ATTENTIVE HEART
THE POWER OF NOW

Let the Quilt Design Inspire a Unique Backing!

Frequently, you will have leftover scraps from making the top of the quilt. Let those scraps, and the quilt design itself, inspire a fun backing for your piece. Lay out your materials on a design wall, cutting them into strips if necessary, to piece a backing that reflects the personality of the quilt top. This is the perfect time to add a label into the mix as well!

Daisy Drop

FINISHED QUILT:
67$\frac{7}{8}$″ × 67$\frac{7}{8}$″

Designers: Natalia Bonner and Kathleen Whiting

Made by Vickie Christensen and Natalia Bonner; quilted by Natalia Bonner; bound by Kathleen Whiting

Three colors—two solids and a simple print—give this quilt a bold, graphic look. Although you can use yardage to make it, this design would easily lend itself to scraps. The blocks are appliquéd and set on point.

Materials

Yardages are based on fabric that is at least 40″ wide.

White: 5 yards

Purple: 2 yards

Yellow: 2 yards

Binding: ⅝ yard of purple fabric

Backing: 4¼ yards

Batting: 96″ wide, 2⅛ yards

Cutting

Use patterns A and B (page 73) as indicated.

Purple

- Cut 108 petals using pattern A.

Yellow

- Cut 120 petals using pattern A.

White

- Cut 13 squares 16½″ × 16½″.
- Cut 2 squares 23⅞″ × 23⅞″; cut in half diagonally twice to make 8 side setting triangles.
- Cut 2 squares 12¼″ × 12¼″; cut in half diagonally to make 4 corner setting triangles.
- From the leftover fabric, cut 13 circles, 8 half-circles, and 4 quarter-circles using pattern B.

Making the Blocks

This quilt is made up of 13 whole blocks, 8 half-blocks, and 4 quarter-blocks.

1. Refer to Appliqué Method (at right). Prepare the purple appliqué pieces A as described.

2. Use a blanket or satin stitch to appliqué 6 purple A petals onto all 13 of the 16½″ × 16½″ blocks. Place the vertical petals first, and then add the others. To ensure exact placement, use the 60° marks on a quilter's ruler or a 60° triangular ruler to place the petals.

3. Appliqué 6 yellow A petals onto all 13 of the 16½″ × 16½″ blocks.

4. Appliqué 3 purple petals onto each of 4 side setting triangles. One petal is perpendicular to one short side of the triangle. Reverse the placement for the remaining 4 side setting triangles to create mirror images setting triangles.

Appliqué Method

Before cutting out the appliqué pieces, spray the fabric with several applications of starch. After each application, press the fabric to ensure it is dry. Repeat until the fabric is stiff.

I use a raw-edge starch method to attach the appliqué pieces, instead of using fusible web. The starch method allows me to cut away the background fabric behind my appliqués after they are applied. The background fabric can often show through an appliqué, especially when the background is darker than the appliqué; cutting away the background helps prevent this show-through. Cutting away also reduces wear in heavy areas and makes for smoother machine quilting.

Cut out the shapes from the starched fabric. Use a water-soluble glue stick on the appliqué piece's edges to glue it in place. Set your machine to a blanket stitch, and stitch around the appliqué piece. There is no need to turn under the edges of the appliqué because the starch prevents fraying while stitching.

Cut out the fabric from behind the appliqué, leaving a ¼″ seam allowance around the appliqué's edges, especially if the underneath fabric is showing through. Be very careful to cut into only the background fabric, which can often show through an appliqué, especially when the background is darker than the appliqué.

Wait until the quilt is quilted and bound before washing out the starch and glue.

5. Appliqué 2 purple petals onto 2 of the smaller corner triangles and 1 petal onto the other 2 corner setting triangles.

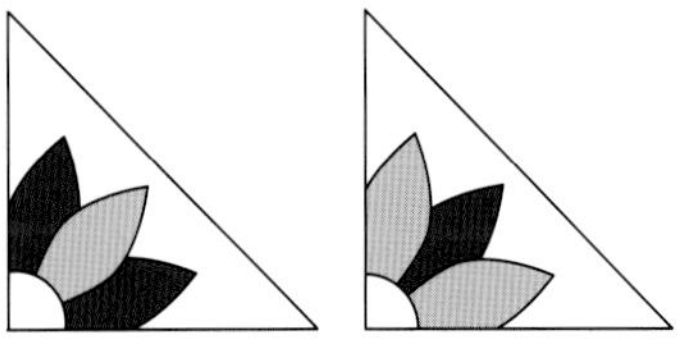

6. Referring to Steps 4 and 5 drawings for placement, appliqué 3 yellow petals onto each of the 8 larger triangles. Appliqué 2 yellow petals onto 2 of the smaller corner triangles and 1 yellow petal onto the other 2 corner triangles.

7. Appliqué the white B circle onto the center of each full block. Appliqué the half-circles and quarter-circles onto the half-blocks and quarter-blocks, respectively.

Putting It All Together

Seam allowances are ¼″ unless otherwise indicated.

1. The blocks are set on point. Sew together the blocks into 7 diagonal rows, as shown in the assembly diagram. Be sure to place the blocks so all the purple petals face in the same direction.

2. Sew together the diagonal rows.

Quilt assembly

Quilting and Finishing

1. Layer and baste the quilt top, batting, and backing.

2. Quilt as desired and bind the quilt.

Interweave

FINISHED QUILT: 60½″ × 82½″

FINISHED BLOCKS: Block A: 6″ × 6″ • Block B: 6″ × 4″ • Block C: 6″ × 5″

Designer: Kim Schaefer

Pieced by Kim Schaefer; quilted by Diane Minkley of Patched Works, Inc.

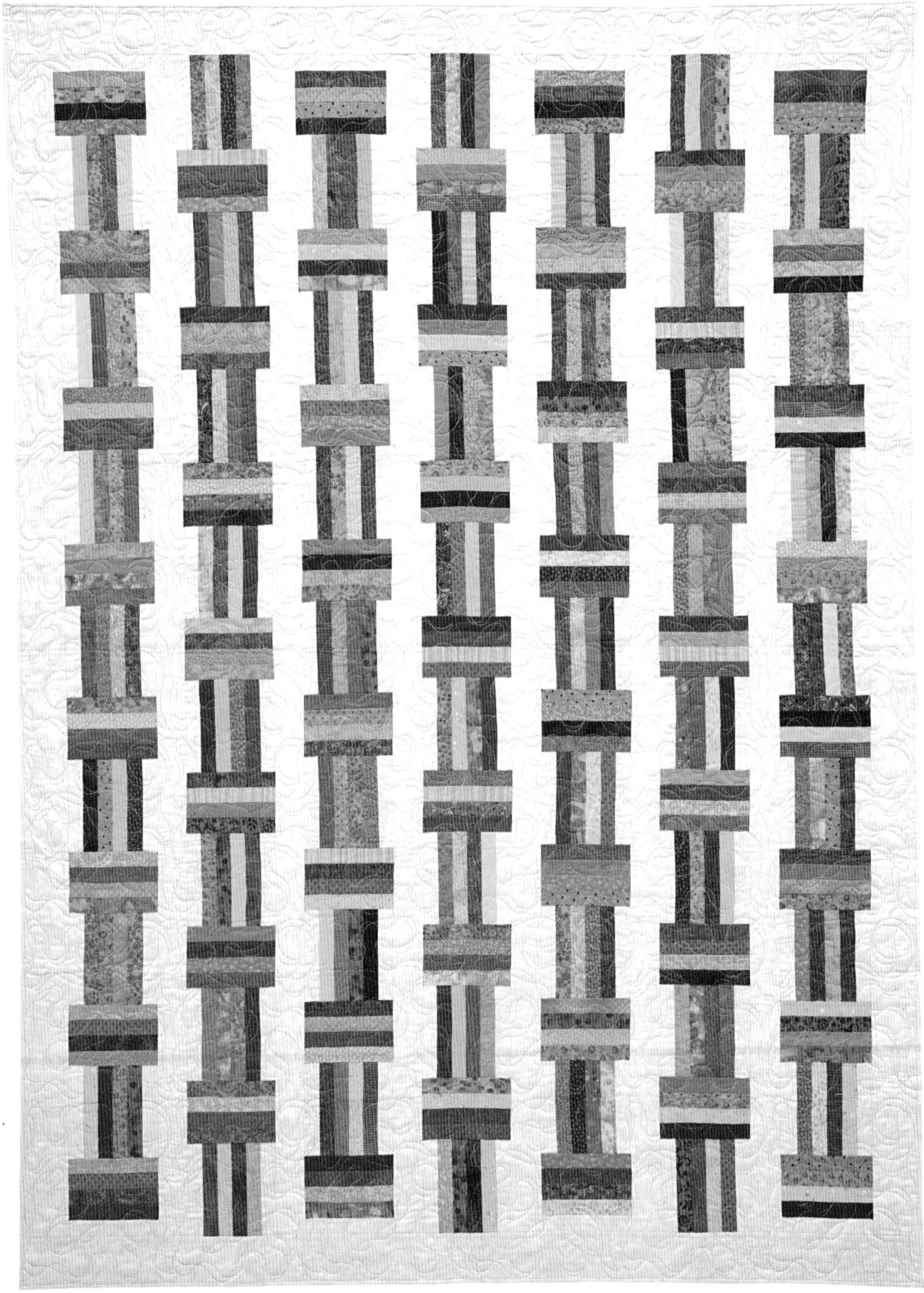

A collection of bright pinks, yellows, and oranges surrounded by a light lattice and border gives this quilt a fresh, cheerful look.

Materials

Assorted pinks, yellows, and oranges: 3½ yards total for pieced blocks

Light: 2¾ yards for pieced blocks, lattice, and border

Backing and binding: 5 yards

Batting: 65″ × 87″

Cutting

Assorted pinks, yellows, and oranges

- Cut a total of 420 rectangles 1½″ × 6½″ for pieced blocks.

Light fabric

- Cut 112 rectangles 1½″ × 6½″ for pieced blocks.
- Cut 6 strips 2½″ × 76½″ for lattice.
- Cut 2 strips 3½″ × 76½″ for side borders.
- Cut 2 strips 3½″ × 60½″ for top and bottom borders.

Piecing

1. Piece Block A. Press. Make 52 blocks.

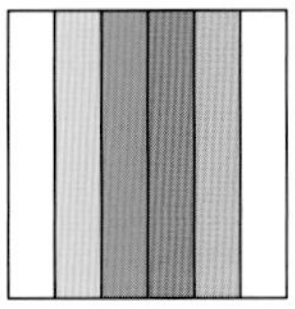

Block A—Make 52.

2. Piece Block B. Press. Make 45 blocks.

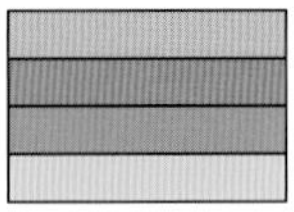

Block B—Make 45.

3. Piece Block C. Press. Make 8 blocks.

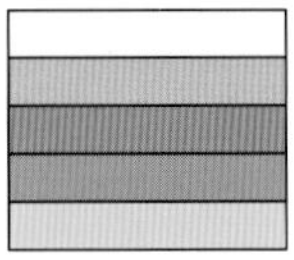

Block C—Make 8.

Putting It All Together

Quilt Center

1. Arrange and sew together the blocks in 7 vertical rows of 15 blocks each. Refer to the quilt assembly diagram as needed. Press.

2. Sew the lattice pieces between the rows to form the quilt top. Press.

Border

1. Sew the 2 side borders to the quilt top. Press toward the borders.

2. Sew the top and bottom borders to the quilt top. Press toward the borders.

Finishing

1. Layer the quilt with batting and backing. Baste or pin.

2. Quilt as desired and bind.

Quilt assembly

Flowered Dishes

FINISHED QUILT: 46⅝″ × 46⅝″ ◆ FINISHED BLOCK: 11″ × 11″

Designer: Alethea Ballard
Made by Alethea Ballard

Dishes is a fabric-lover's delight. It has large spaces that can accommodate large images or appliqué. The visual interplay of the patterns, colors, and fabrics creates a dramatic effect and is exciting to look at. • Putting the curved pieces together is a delightful way to play with big flowers and bright colors. The crosses in the centers serve both as a frame and a visual balance. They create repetition and give the design structure. Bright or bold colors will really stand out, while quieter colors will recede. Whatever fabric theme you use, the results are exciting, surprising, and satisfying. • The construction of this quilt is a little tricky and requires some experience. That said, when you do have all the fussy curve-pieced blocks made, the top goes together fast. With no borders—just thirteen blocks and the setting triangles—you can put it together quickly, and you're off to quilting.

Materials

Flower print: 2+ yards total of a variety of fabrics or 36 pieces 7″ × 7″ for convex (A) pieces (Extra fabric is allotted for fussy cutting flower motifs.)

Contrasting fabrics: 1¾ yards total of a variety of fabrics or 36 pieces 7″ × 7″ for concave (B) pieces and leaves (C) (I cut the leaves using leftovers from the concave pieces.)

Solids: ⅓ yard each of 3 different fabrics for block crosses (Choose fabrics with good contrast to the curve blocks.)

Neutral or large motif: ⅞ yard (or more if the large motif needs fussy cutting) for alternate blocks

Medium-motif print: ⅓ yard for alternate-block triangles

Medium- or small-motif print: ⅓ yard for side setting triangle corners

Large-motif print: 1 yard for setting triangles

Binding: ½ yard

Backing: 3 yards

Batting: 53″ × 53″

Template plastic

Fusible web

TIP *Try a couple of practice Drunkard's Path blocks to get your rhythm and to work out any issues. It also helps you see how the fabrics are looking together, so you can make changes before you get too far into the project.*

Cutting

Flower print

- Cut 36 convex A pieces (see Drunkard's Path Units, page 24).

Contrasting fabrics

- Cut 36 concave B pieces (see Drunkard's Path Units, page 24).
- Cut 12 leaves from leftover concave pieces (*optional*: see Alternate Blocks, page 26).

Solids

- Cut 1 strip 4¾″ × width of fabric from each of the 3 fabrics. Subcut the strip into 3 strips 4½″ × 13″ for the cross bars.
- Cut 2 strips 1½″ × width of fabric from each of the 3 fabrics. Subcut the strips into a total of 4 strips 1½″ × 13″ for the cross ends and centers.

Neutral or large motif

- Fussy cut 4 rectangles 8⅞″ × 16¾″ for the alternate blocks.

Medium-motif print

- Cut 4 squares 6¼″ × 6¼″. Subcut each square in half diagonally for the alternate block triangles.

Medium- or small-motif print

- Cut 4 squares 5½″ × 5½″. Subcut each square in half diagonally for the border setting triangle.

Large-motif print

- Cut 2 squares 9¾″ × 9¾″. Subcut each square in half diagonally for the corner triangles.
- Cut 3 strips 5½″ × width of fabric for the border setting polygon.

Binding

- Cut 6 strips 2½″ × width of fabric.

NOTE

Use That Fabric: Large Florals

Cutting large florals off-centered and pairing them up leads to such wonderful visual treats.

Blocks

Use ¼″ seam allowances unless otherwise noted.

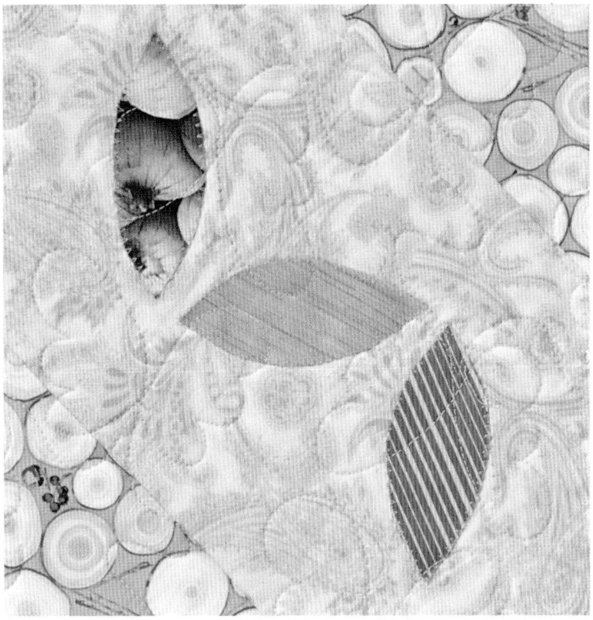

Make Templates

Make templates by tracing patterns A, B, and optional C (page 74) onto template plastic. Mark the ¼″ seam allowances and grainlines on the templates to help cut the pieces and accurately sew them together. Cut out the plastic templates.

Drunkard's Path Units

Each Drunkard's Path unit consists of a convex A and a concave B piece. You will need 36 blocks.

1. Trace 36 templates A and B onto the right side of the corresponding fabrics. Position the corners of the templates on the grainlines so that the curves will be on the bias, giving you the flexibility needed to sew the curve. Position and trace template A on the fabric so that the flower designs are well within the ¼″ seam allowance. Draw around the template with a pencil, then rotary cut the straight corners, and use scissors to cut the curves.

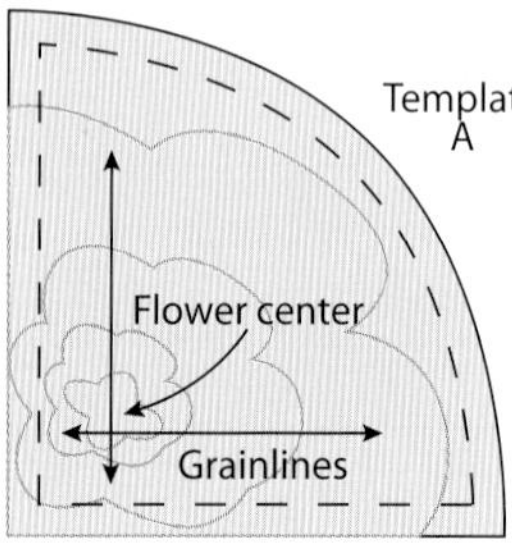

Cut convex (A) pieces with flower centers inside the ¼″ seam allowance.

2. Arrange the convex A and concave B pieces into 36 paired sets. Pair fabrics to provide a pleasing arrangement of values and contrast in the block design.

3. Clip the B pieces along the seam allowance, beginning and ending about 1″ from the edges. Make the clips less than ¼″ deep and about ¼″ apart. Careful clipping in the seam on the concave side of the block will help make the sewing successful.

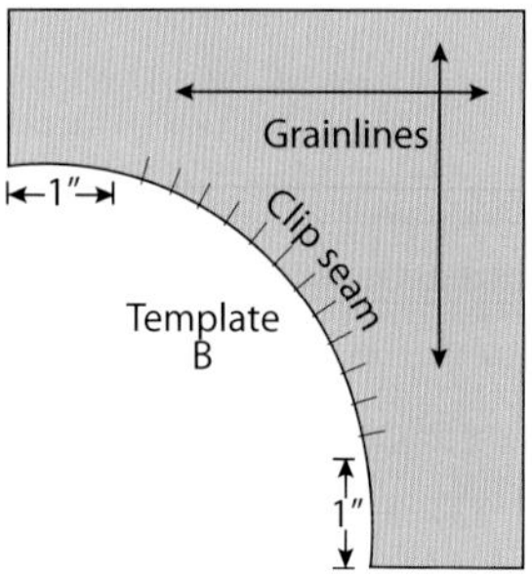

Clip concave seam allowance a scant ¼″ deep and ¼″ apart.

4. Fold both pieces in half, aligning the straight edges, and finger-press the curved edge at the fold to mark the middle.

5. Place the concave B piece onto its corresponding convex A piece, right sides together, and pin the center.

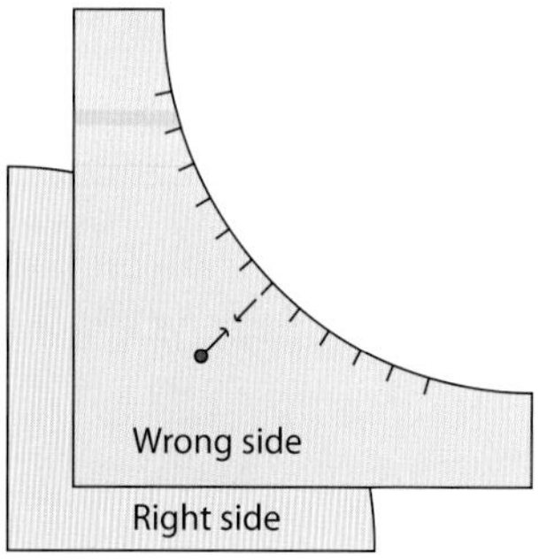

Pin center of curve.

6. Pin the rest of the seam.

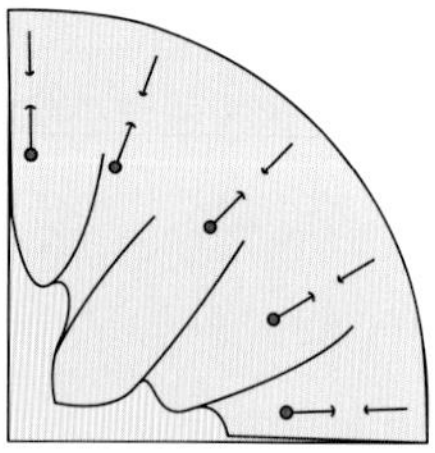

Pin seam.

7. Sew the seam. Use a stiletto to keep the edges of the seams even.

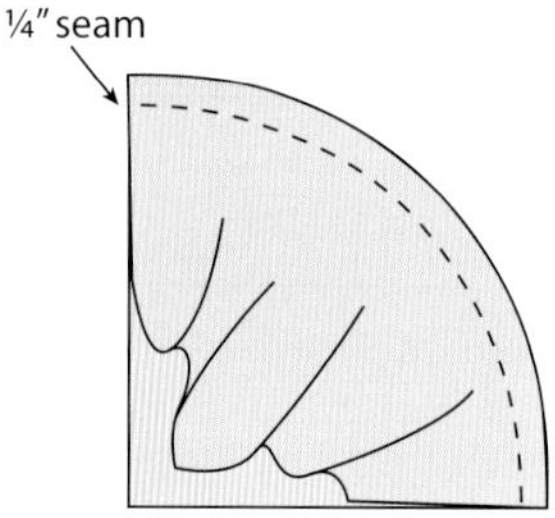

Sew seam.

8. Press the seam gently toward the concave B piece.

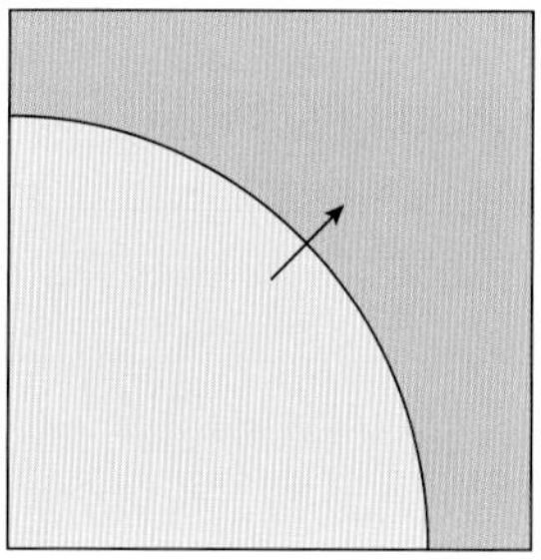

Press toward concave B piece.

9. Trim to 5½″ × 5½″, if necessary. Make 36.

Cross Units

Arrange the cross block fabrics into 3 sets. Each set will contain 3 strips 4½″ × 13″ for bars, 3 strips 1½″ × 13″ for ends, and 1 strip 1½″ × 13″ for the center. Label the sets Cross #1, Cross #2, and Cross #3. Work with one set of fabrics at a time, starting with Cross #1.

1. Sew 1 end strip 1½″ × 13″ to each 4½″ × 13″ bar strip to make 3 strip sets. Press.

2. Cut 1 strip set into 8 pieces 1½″ wide for the single-post units.

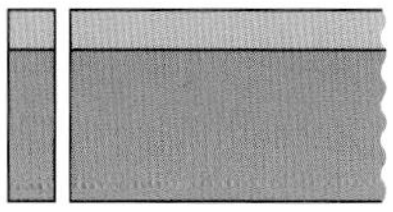

1½″

Cut single-post units.

3. Sew the remaining 2 strip sets to each long side of the 1½″ × 13″ center strip to make a double-post strip set. Press.

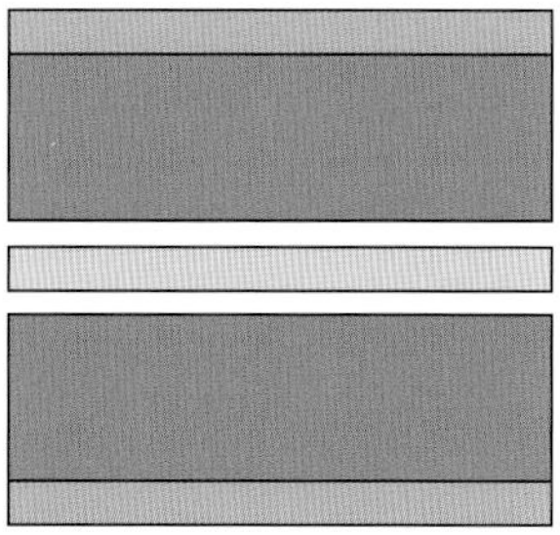

Make double-post strip set.

4. Cut the double-post strip set into 4 pieces 1½″ wide for the double-post units.

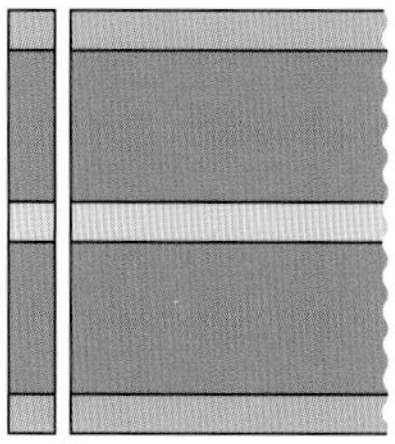

1½″

Cut double-post units.

5. At this point there are 4 double-post units and 8 single-post units from Cross #1. This is enough to make 4 matching Cross blocks. Repeat Steps 1–4 with the remaining sets of fabrics to make the following:

Cross #2: Make 6 single-post units and 3 double-post units for 3 matching cross blocks.

Cross #3: Make 4 single-post units and 2 double-post units for 2 matching cross blocks.

Drunkard's Path Cross Block

1. Sew a single-post unit between 2 Drunkard's Path units, keeping the end piece to the outside edge. Make 18 sets of half-blocks. Press.

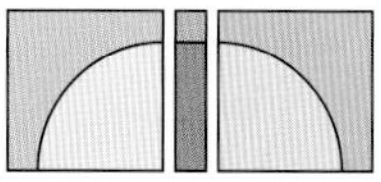

Make 18 half-blocks.

2. Sew a double-post unit between 2 half-blocks, aligning the center seams. Press. Make 9 blocks.

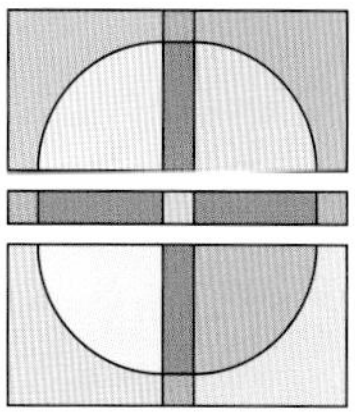

Block assembly—make 9.

Alternate Blocks

1. Fold and press each 8⅞″ × 16¾″ rectangle in half, right sides together, along the long side.

2. Fold and press each alternate block triangle in half, right sides together, from the point to the center of the long side.

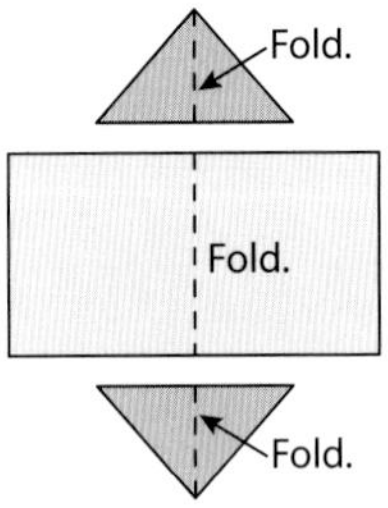

Fold rectangles and triangles in half.

3. Align the center folds and pin the triangles to the rectangles, right sides together. Sew the triangles to the sides of the rectangles. Press.

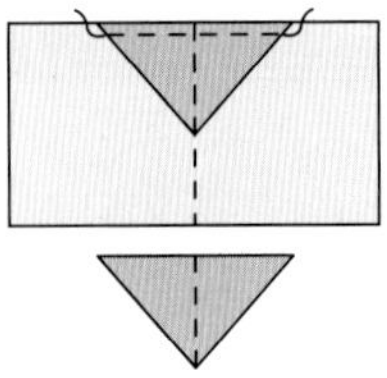

Sew triangles to rectangles.

4. Using the side triangles as corners, cut off the tips of the rectangles to create a 12″ × 12″ square. Make 4.

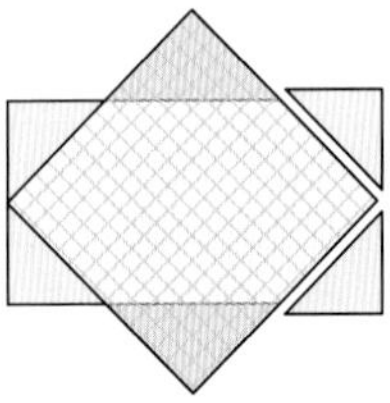

Trim off rectangle tips.

5. *Optional*: Trace 12 leaves onto the leaf fabric, using template C (see Make Templates, page 24). Fuse and topstitch the leaves onto the alternate block using raw-edge or fused-edge appliqué.

Side Setting Triangles

1. Remove the selvage edges from the 3 strips 5½″ wide and sew them together end to end. Press the seams open.

2. Cut 8 polygon shapes with the long side measuring 17½″. Place the ruler on the fabric and use the 45° mark to create the correct angle.

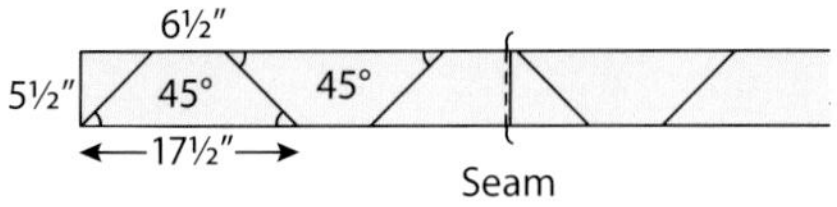

Cut border setting polygons.

3. Fold and press the polygons in half, right sides together, along the long edge and aligning angled edges.

4. Fold and press the setting triangle in half, right sides together, from the point to the center of the long side.

5. Align the center folds, right sides together, and pin the triangle to the short, straight side of the polygon. Sew the triangle to the polygon. Press toward the polygon. (*Note: An accurate ¼″ seam allowance is necessary to piece the shapes into a setting triangle.*) Trim the triangle tips. Make 8.

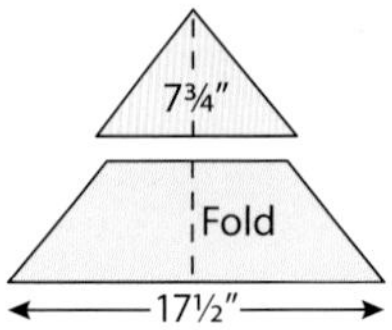

Border setting triangles—make 8.

Quilt Assembly

1. Sew the blocks and side setting triangles together in diagonal rows following the quilt assembly diagram. The setting triangles are oversize.

2. Press the rows and trim off the triangle tips that stick out beyond the edges.

3. Sew the rows together.

4. Press and trim to square up and remove any last triangle points.

5. Sew on the corner triangles, and trim to square up with the edges of the quilt top. Press.

Finishing

Layer, quilt, and bind your quilt.

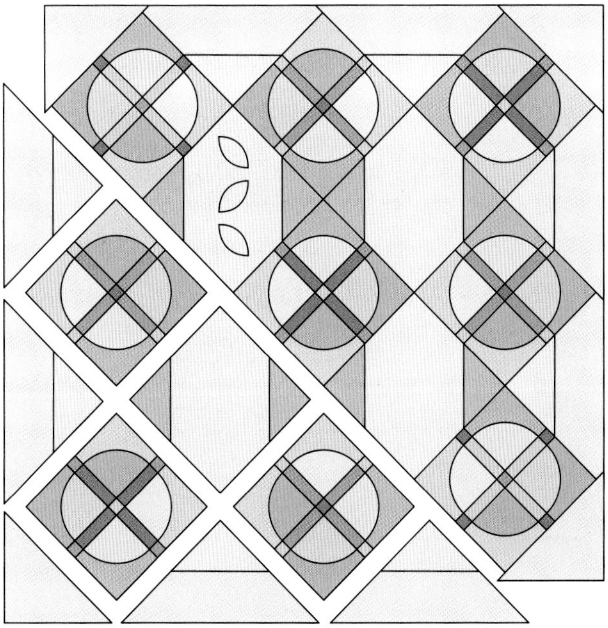

Quilt assembly

Option: Change the Alternate Blocks

Asian Dishes, 58½″ × 58½″, made by Alethea Ballard, machine quilting by Elaine Beatty

The large space in the center blocks is a natural spot to showcase some amazing fabric. In this quilt, I used the beautiful women and the gorgeous house to create visual focal points. The luscious blues and rich ombrés—fabrics that gradually change color across the width of the yardage—called out to be used. Using ombrés created wonderful, subtle color variations. Playing with the floral fabrics and the placement of the matching stems and flowers resulted in a lovely, elegant wallhanging.

Detail of *Asian Dishes*

City Lights

FINISHED QUILT: 65″ × 73″
FINISHED BLOCK: 7″ × 21″

Designer: Cherri House
Machine pieced and quilted by Cherri House

Each day, as thousands of commuters—myself included—drive in the early morning darkness into downtown Houston, the buildings, lit from within, are a welcome greeting. In this quilt the blocks—black, alternating with mainly pastels—are the lighted windows of the building. I've used color to create windows where some lights are out and where some are dimmed. Place the medium pastels and the charcoals randomly throughout the black units to give depth and variety to your office building.

Materials

Black: 3¾ yards for pieced blocks, sashing, and binding

Variety of pale pastels: 1¾ yards for blocks

Variety of medium pastels (3 or more): ⅛ yard of each fabric for blocks

Charcoal gray: ⅛ yard for blocks

Backing: 4⅛ yards

Batting: 73″ × 81″

Cutting

Black

- Cut 10 strips 7½″ × width of fabric.

  Subcut into 3½″ × 7½″ rectangles for a total of 108 rectangles.

- Cut 17 strips 1½″ × width of fabric.
- Cut 8 strips 2¼″ × width of fabric.

Pale pastels

- Cut 14 strips 3½″ × width of fabric.

  Subcut into 3½″ × 7½″ rectangles for a total of 70 rectangles; subcut 8 of these rectangles (in various colors) into 2 strips 1½″ × 7½″, for a total of 16 strips.

Medium pastels

- Cut 3 strips 3½″ × width of fabric.

  Subcut into 15 rectangles 3½″ × 7½″; subcut 1 of these rectangles into 2 strips 1½″ × 7½″.

Charcoal gray

- Cut 1 strip 3½″ × width of fabric.

  Subcut into 5 rectangles 3½″ × 7½″.

Block Assembly

Each block contains 4 black rectangles 3½″ × 7½″ and 3 pastel (and an occasional charcoal gray) rectangles 3½″ × 7½″. There are 27 blocks in this quilt.

Refer to the quilt assembly diagram (next page). To give some perspective and color balance throughout the entire quilt, it is recommended that you use a design wall or the floor to arrange the fabric pieces before sewing the blocks. To make each block, sew 4 black 3½″ × 7½″ rectangles and 3 pastel 3½″ × 7½″ rectangles together as shown. Use a charcoal gray rectangle in place of a pastel piece in 5 blocks. Sew a total of 27 blocks, and press all seams toward the black fabric.

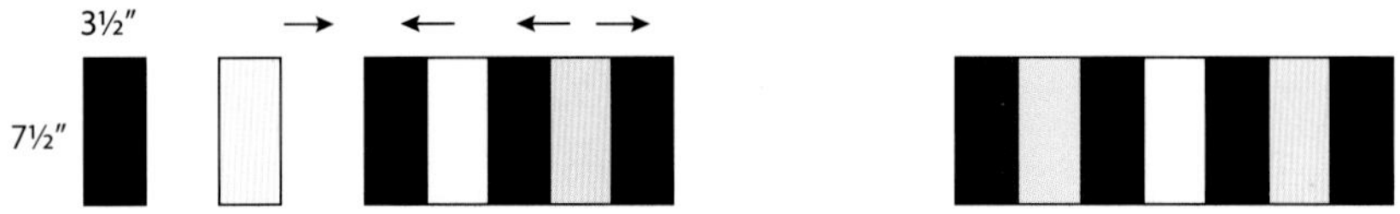

Make 22.

Make 5.

Quilt Construction

This quilt has 9 rows with sashing strips between the rows.

1. Refer to the quilt assembly diagram to arrange the prepared blocks on a design wall or the floor, in a configuration of 3 blocks in a row across and 9 rows down. Think of the blocks creating 3 vertical columns of "windows" in a building. Rearrange if necessary to evenly distribute the blocks with the medium pastels and darkened "windows." Place pastel 1½″ × 7½″ sashing strips between the blocks in each row, again referring to the quilt assembly diagram.

2. Sew each of the 9 rows together, and press the seams toward the black fabric. Return the rows to the design wall in their original location, leaving about 3″ between each row.

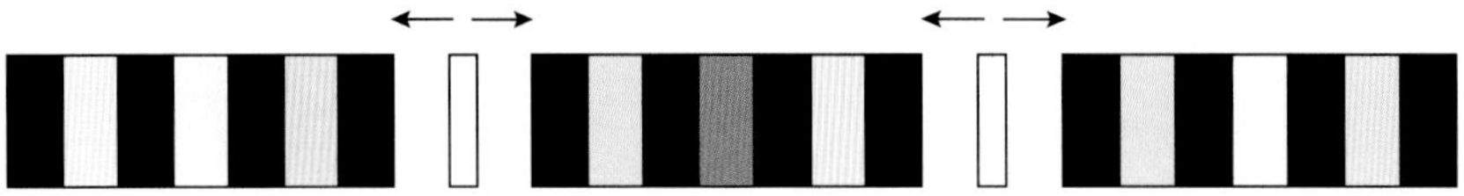

Make 9.

3. Use the black 1½″ strips to make 10 sashing strips, 1½″ × 65½″, sewing the strips together and trimming as needed. Place a sashing strip between each row on the design wall and a sashing strip at the top and bottom of the quilt.

4. To ensure alignment of the window units, pin each row and sashing strip from the outer edge of the row first, then pin at the center, and then at multiple spaces in between. Check that the "windows" are all in line before sewing the rows. As you sew the rows and sashing strips together, have the sashing strip against the feed dogs of your machine. Make sure that as you sew over the seam allowances they stay flat. Press the seams toward the sashing strips.

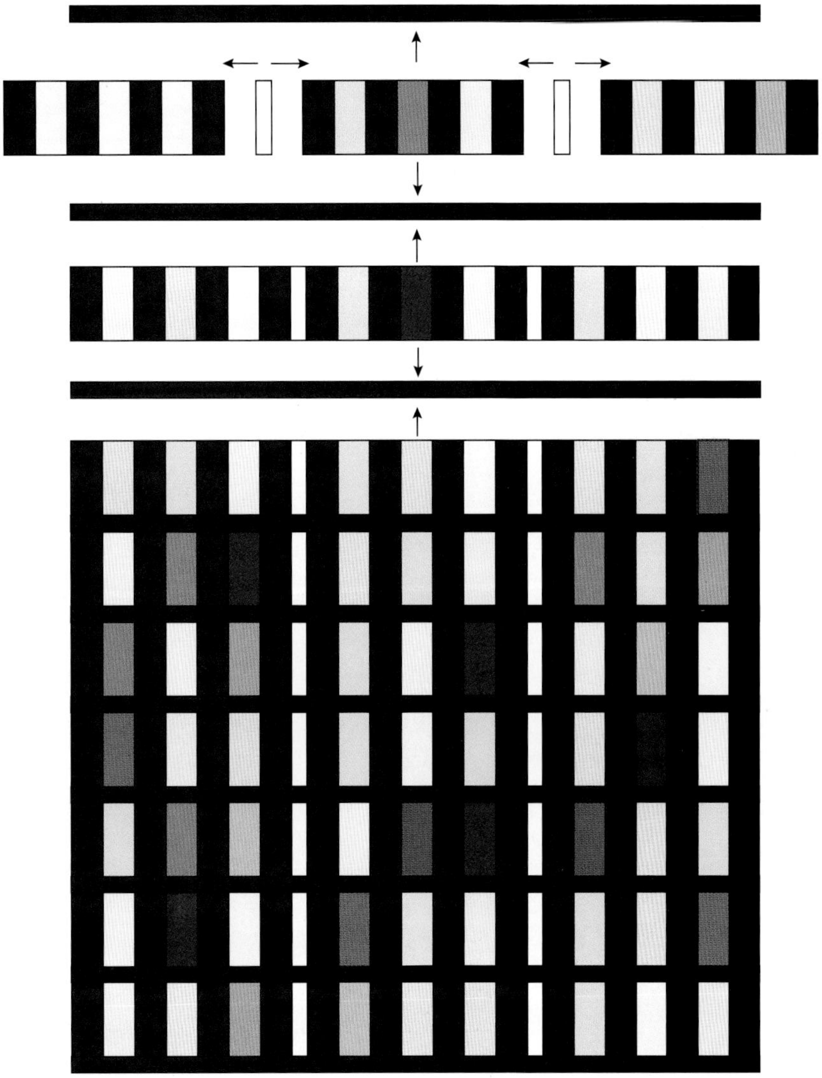

Quilt assembly

Finish

Layer, quilt, and bind your quilt. Use the black 2¼″ strips for the binding.

Circle

FINISHED QUILT: 51″ × 51″ ◆ FINISHED BLOCK: 5½″ × 5½″

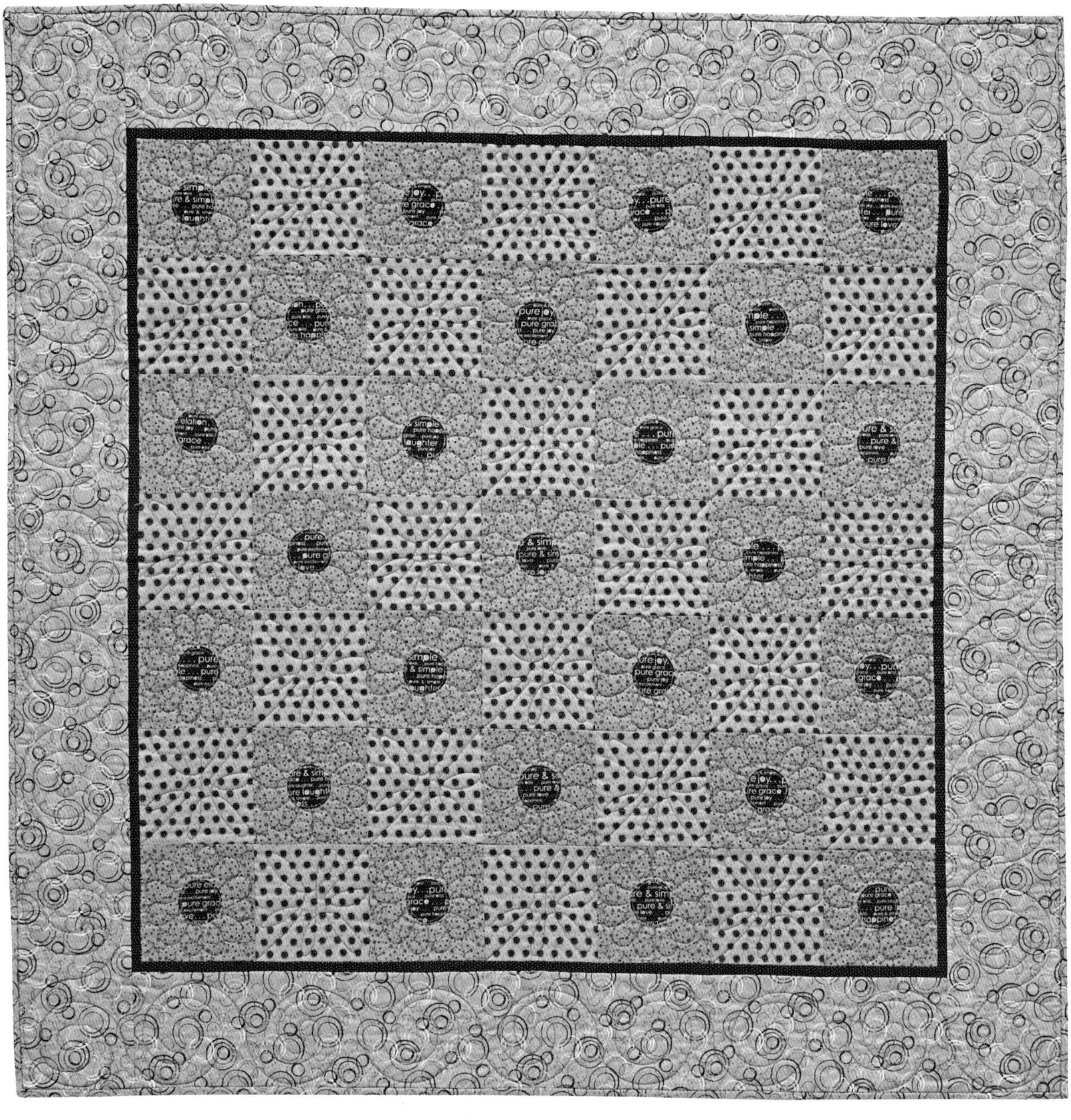

Designer: Sweetwater

Made by Sweetwater; machine quilted by Brian Clements

The blue and brown color palette of this quilt is so calming, especially on a crisp fall day. For a different variation, try a summer version using brighter fabrics. Make the circles pop even more by using a light-colored neutral background behind colorful circles. Think citrus shades—orange, lime green, and pink.

Materials

Circle and plain blocks: 2 different prints, 1 yard each

Circle block dots: ¼ yard

Inner border: ¼ yard

Outer border and binding: 1⅜ yards

Paper-backed fusible web: ½ yard

Backing: 59″ × 59″

Batting: 59″ × 59″

Instructions

Use the circle appliqué pattern (page 73) as indicated below; ¼″ seam allowance is included when constructing blocks and borders.

Blocks

This quilt has 25 circle appliquéd blocks and 24 plain blocks.

1. Cut 25 squares 6″ × 6″ from the circle block fabric.

2. Cut 24 squares 6″ × 6″ from the plain block fabric.

3. To make the appliqués, make a template from the circle pattern and trace around it 25 times on the paper side of the fusible web.

4. Iron the fusible web to the wrong side of the dot fabric, following the manufacturer's instructions.

5. Cut out the circles on the traced lines.

6. Peel off the paper backing and iron a circle to the center of each of the 25 circle block squares.

7. Machine stitch close to the edge of each circle, using a straight stitch.

Quilt Top

There are 7 rows of 7 blocks each. Refer to the quilt assembly diagram.

1. Begin the first row with a circle appliqué block. With right sides together, sew 7 squares together, alternating appliqué and plain blocks, to make 1 row. Press all the seams toward the circle appliquéd blocks. Repeat 3 times.

2. Sew another row of 7 squares, starting this time with a plain block, alternating plain and appliqué blocks. Press. Repeat 2 times.

3. Sew the 7 rows together and press.

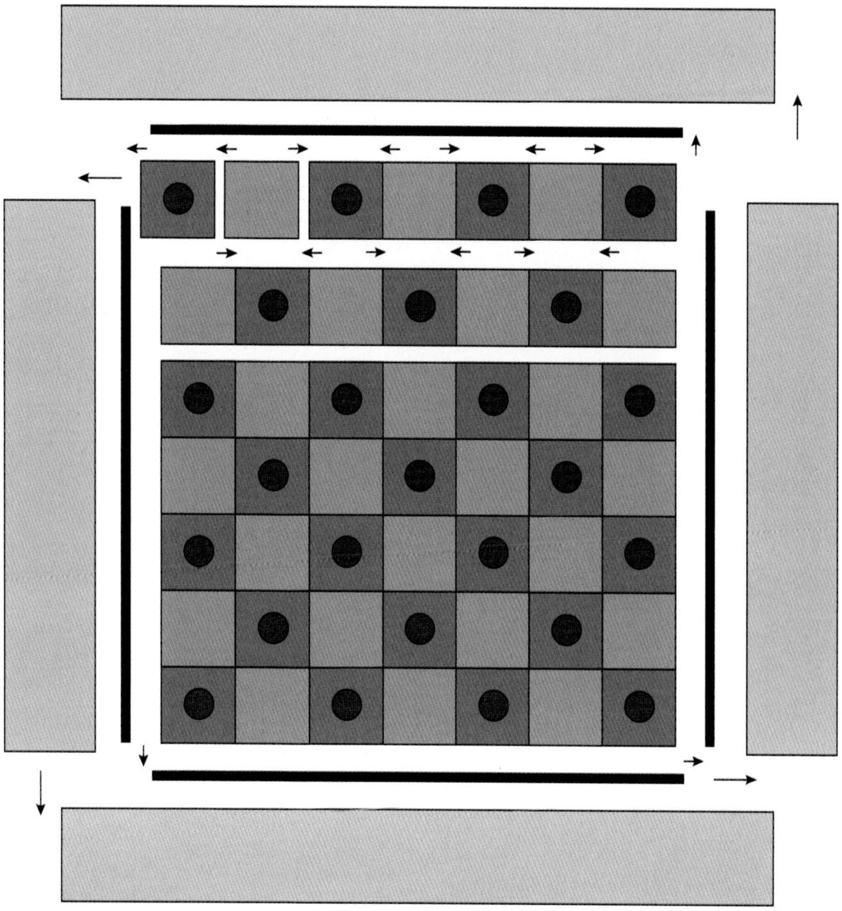

Quilt assembly

Borders

This quilt has an inner border and an outer border. Sew the strips to the sides first, and then the top and bottom of the quilt.

1. Cut 4 strips 1″ × the width of the fabric for the inner border.

2. Cut 5 strips 6″ × the width of the fabric for the outer border.

Photo by Farmhouse Creations, Inc.

Finishing

For the binding, cut 6 strips 2¼″ × the width of the fabric; sew them together using diagonal seams to make 1 long strip.

Layer, quilt, and bind the quilt.

Quilt your quilt top as desired. Our quilt features a flower pattern around each appliquéd circle and free-flowing swirls on the border and in the plain blocks.

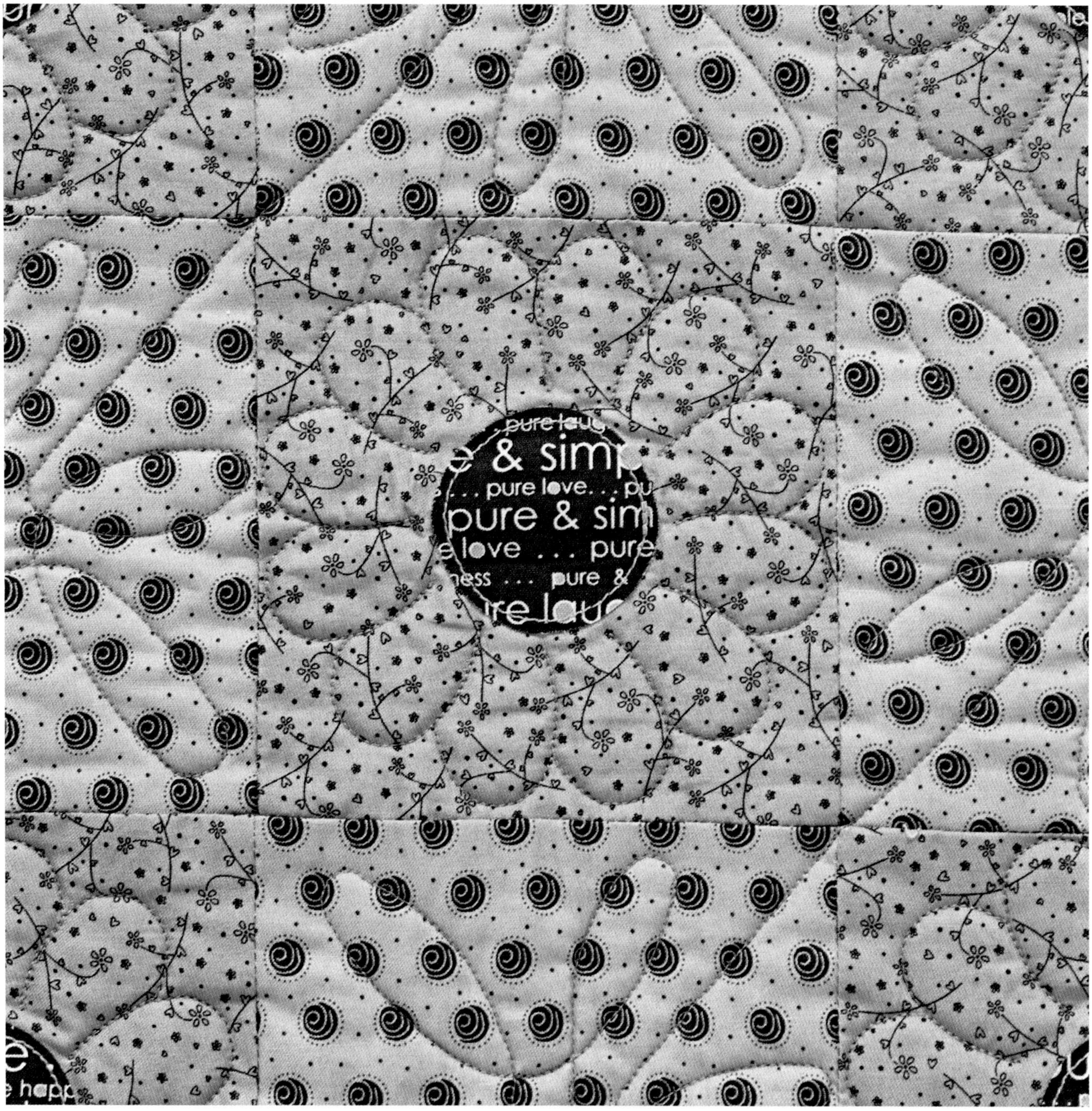

Lake Shore Drive

FINISHED QUILT: 57″ × 72″ ◆ FINISHED BLOCK: 5″ × 9″

Designer: Amy Walsh

Anyone who knows me knows how much I love, love, love Chicago. One of my favorite drives to take in the city is down Lake Shore Drive, especially on a sunny day. Lake Michigan is on one side and the beautiful skyline is on the other. This particular color palette is my picture of Lake Shore Drive on a clear winter day. The different shades of blue suggest the sky and frozen water, as does the addition of white.

Materials

Assorted coordinating small-scale prints: 20 strips 3″ × 42″ (or 1¾ yards total) for pieced Four-Patch blocks

Large-scale print: 2¼ yards for alternate 8½″ strips

Binding: ½ yard

Backing: 3¾ yards

Batting: 67″ × 82″

TIP *This quilt is perfect for any of the larger prints you want to work with—especially those that you love too much to cut up. Choose prints for the pieced blocks that match the colors in your alternate print. And, as always, the more prints the better. We used about 30 for the pictured quilt.*

Cutting

Assorted coordinating small-scale prints

- Cut 20 strips 3″ × 42″.

  Subcut each 3″ strip into 8 rectangles 3″ × 5″.

Large-scale print

- Cut 4 strips 8½″ × length of fabric (parallel to the selvage).
  Note: These strips will be trimmed to fit later.

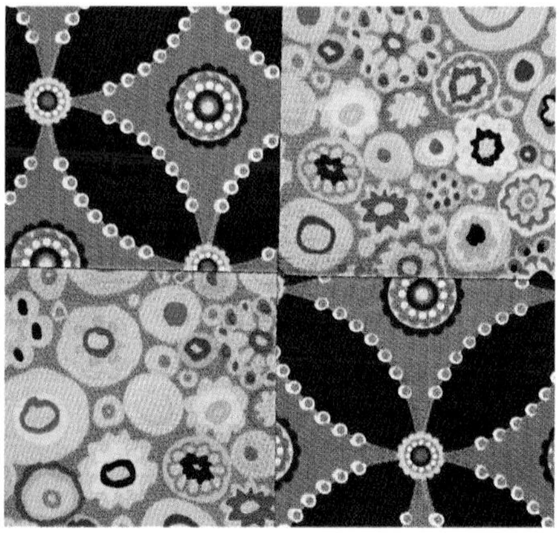

Piecing and Pressing

Each Lake Shore Drive block is essentially a Four-Patch constructed with 2 rectangles from 2 different fabrics. You can change the way this quilt looks by piecing your rectangles from 4 different fabrics, giving the quilt a scrappier look.

1. Sew 2 sets of 2 rectangles together. Press the seams open as you sew.

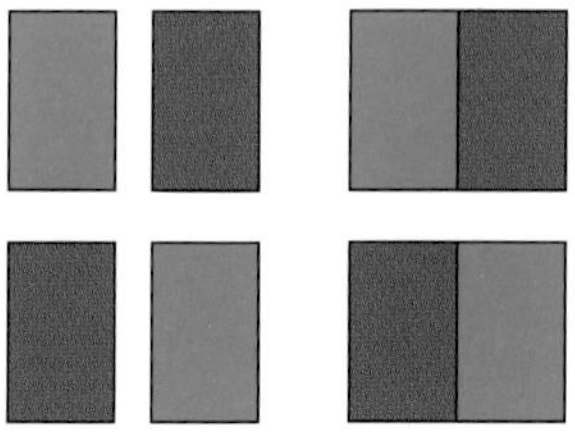

2. Sew the resulting 2 units together. Press the seams open.

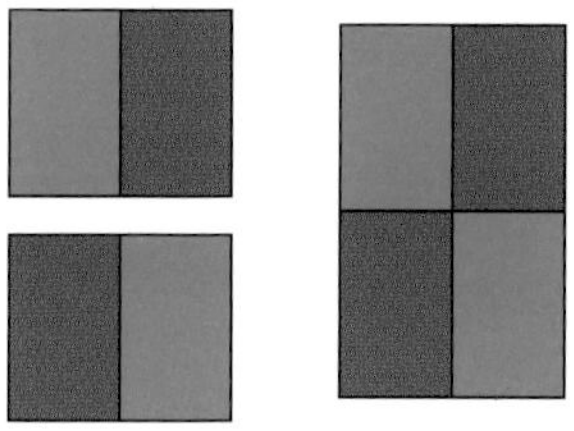

3. Make a total of 40 Four-Patch blocks to make the pictured quilt.

TIP *We always make more blocks than we need so that we have options when we are putting the quilt together. For this particular quilt, an extra couple of blocks will be helpful when laying out your quilt.*

Quilt Top Construction

When you have completed the blocks, arrange them in 5 rows alternating with the 8½″ strips. Each row should have 8 Four-Patch blocks. Refer to the quilt assembly diagram as needed. When you find an arrangement you like, sew the Four-Patch blocks together in vertical rows and measure the length of the four-patch rows. Trim the 8½″ strips to that length. Then sew all rows together, pressing the seams open as you sew.

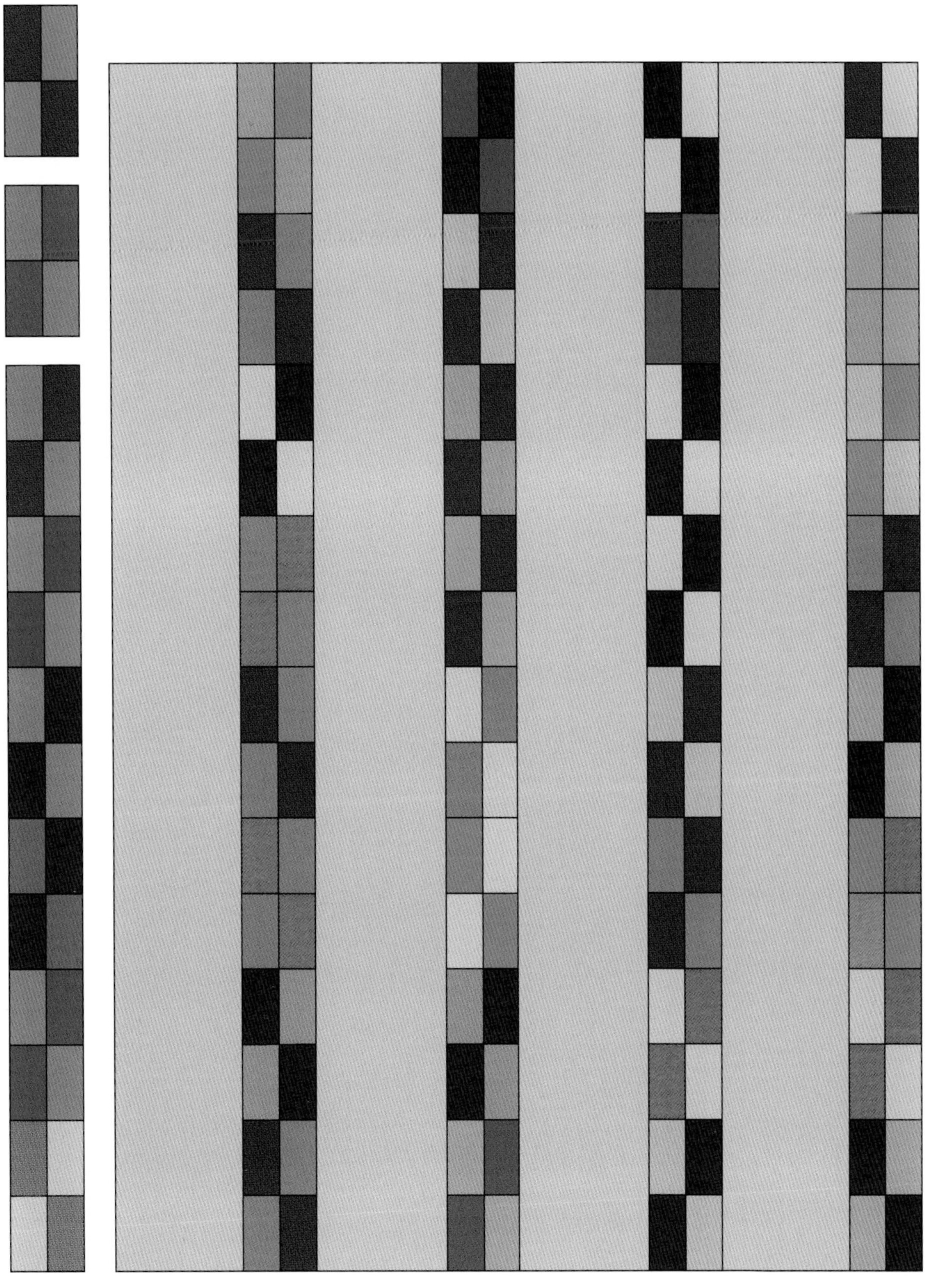

Quilt assembly

Finishing

Layer, quilt, and bind your quilt.

All the Above

FINISHED QUILT: 90″ × 90″ ◆ FINISHED BLOCK: 6″ × 6″

Designer: Amy Walsh
Machine pieced by Amy Walsh; machine quilted by Ann Davidson

I have always loved a basic checkerboard design. This quilt came about one day as I was drawing some checkerboard patterns in my design notebook and trying to find ways to vary them slightly. It's extremely striking and makes a great quilt for guys and girls alike. I happen to love quilts that are constructed with alternate solid blocks. Not only do they look smashing, but they also come together very quickly!

Materials

The yardage given here makes a queen-size quilt. (For other size quilts, refer to Alternate Sizes and Yardage Requirements, next page.)

Note: I used 30 of Marcia Derse's prints from Troy fabrics in the pictured quilt to add plenty of color variation.

Pieced blocks

Assorted prints or colored solids: 19 strips 2¼″ × 40″ or 1¼ yards

Cream-colored solid: 2¾ yards

Solid alternate blocks

Charcoal gray solid: 3⅝ yards

Other

Backing: 8⅓ yards

Batting: 100″ × 100″

Binding: ⅞ yard

Cutting

The cutting amounts are for a queen-size quilt. For other size quilts, refer to Alternate Sizes and Yardage Requirements (next page).

Assorted prints or batiks

- Cut 19 strips 2¼″ × 40″.

  Subcut each strip into 6 rectangles 2¼″ × 6½″ (Unit B). You need a total of 112 Unit B pieces.

Cream solid

- Cut 14 strips 6½″ × 40″.

  Subcut each strip into 8 rectangles 4¾″ × 6½″ (Unit A). You need a total of 112 Unit A pieces.

Charcoal gray solid

- Cut 19 strips 6½″ × 40″.

  Subcut each strip into 6 squares 6½″ × 6½″. You need a total of 113 solid alternate blocks.

ALTERNATE SIZES AND YARDAGE REQUIREMENTS

Quilt size	Block set	Number of pieced blocks	Number of gray solid blocks	Minimum number of print strips	Cream solid	Gray solid	Backing	Batting	Binding
Baby/wall 42″ × 42″	7 × 7	24	25	4 strips 2¼″ × 40″	3 strips 6½″ × 40″ (or ¾ yard)	5 strips 6½″ × 42″ (or 1⅛ yards)	3 yards	52″ × 52″	½ yard
Throw 66″ × 66″	11 × 11	60	61	10 strips 2¼″ × 40″	8 strips 6½″ × 40″ (or 1⅝ yards)	11 strips 6½″ × 40″ (or 2¼ yards)	4¼ yards	76″ × 76″	⅝ yard
Twin 78″ × 78″	13 × 13	84	85	14 strips 2¼″ × 40″	11 strips 6½″ × 40″ (or 2¼ yards)	15 strips 6½″ × 40″ (or 3 yards)	5 yards (44″ wide)	88″ × 88″	¾ yard
King 114″ × 114″	19 × 19	180	181	30 strips 2¼″ × 40″	23 strips 6½″ × 40″ (or 4⅓ yards)	31 strips 6½″ × 40″ (or 5⅞ yards)	10⅓ yards (42″ wide)	124″ × 124″	1 yard

Piecing and Pressing

For this queen-size quilt, you need to make a total of 112 pieced All the Above blocks.

For each pieced block, join a Unit A to a Unit B. Press the seams open. The raw pieced blocks measure 6½″ × 6½″.

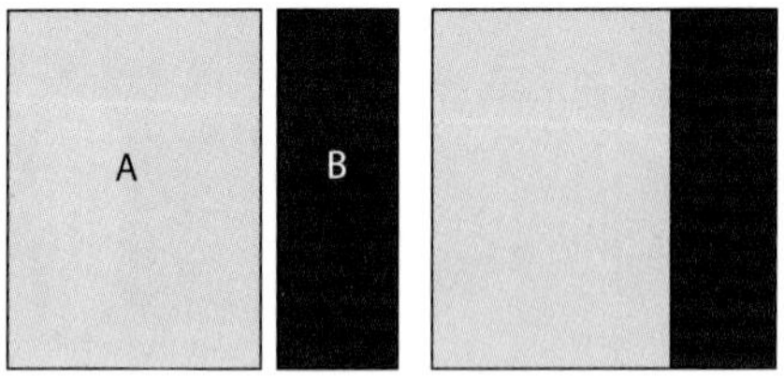

Quilt Top Construction

1. Arrange the pieced blocks alternately with the solid blocks on a design wall or the floor in 15 rows of 15 blocks each. Try to keep the viewer's eye moving constantly around the quilt top by varying the placement of textures and colors in the pieced blocks, keeping the blocks oriented the same way.

2. When you find an arrangement you like, sew the blocks together in rows, pressing the seams open as you sew.

3. Sew the rows together. Press the seams open.

Quilt assembly

Finishing

Layer, quilt, and bind the quilt.

Shake It Up!

Change the look of *All the Above* by using one or more of the following options.

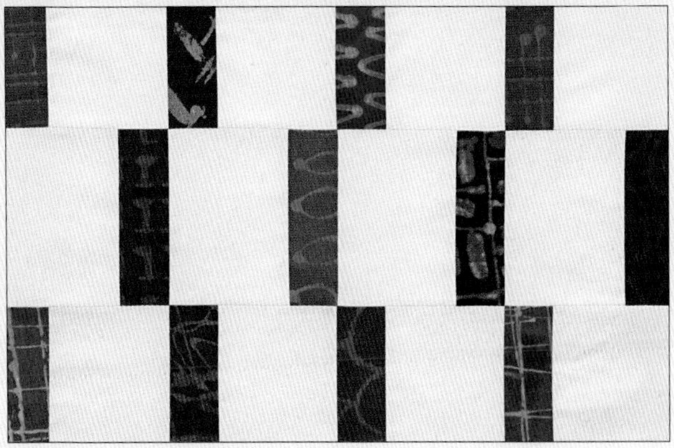

Option 1: Use only pieced blocks and set them alternately, and reverse the direction of alternate rows.

Option 2: Scale down the size of the block, use only pieced blocks, and set them so that the narrow rectangles are facing each other. The finished block size in this sample is 3½″ × 3½″.

Option 3: Using only pieced blocks, set them in horizontal rows, creating a straight line of secondary color. In this example, we used blue florals with red for high contrast.

Retro

FINISHED QUILT: 60″ × 72″ ◆ FINISHED BLOCK: 12″ × 12″

Designer: Camille Roskelley
Pieced and quilted by Camille Roskelley

My great-grandma Ruby was quite a character. At a whopping 5′1″ tall, she had bright red hair and drove a sporty orange Nova in her 70s. That sums her up pretty well. She was a fireball! We used one of her favorite aqua flower brooches, a vintage necklace I found at a flea market, and several classic prints from her fabric collection as the inspiration for the Ruby fabric line. It absolutely had to include red, aqua, and a bit of orange to commemorate the Nova. The same concepts apply to the quilt. Keep it simple and retro, aqua and white, with a little Ruby spunk thrown in. Just for fun.

Materials

Yardages are based on 42″-wide fabric.

Aqua: 2½ yards for blocks

White: 2½ yards for blocks

Red: 1 fat quarter for accent block*

Backing: 3⅞ yards

Binding: ⅝ yard

Cotton batting: 64″ × 76″

** If you decide to skip the red block and make them all aqua, there is enough yardage to do so.*

Cutting

WOF = width of fabric

Aqua

- Cut 11 strips 3½″ × WOF; subcut squares 3½″ × 3½″ (11 per strip, for a total of 116).
- Cut 5 strips 6⅞″ × WOF; subcut squares 6⅞″ × 6⅞″ (6 per strip, for a total of 29).

White

- Cut 11 strips 3½″ × WOF; subcut squares 3½″ × 3½″ (11 per strip, for a total of 120).
- Cut 5 strips 6⅞″ × WOF; subcut squares 6⅞″ × 6⅞″ (6 per strip, for a total of 30).

Red

- Cut 4 squares 3½″ × 3½″.
- Cut 1 square 6⅞″ × 6⅞″.

Binding

- Cut 7 strips 2½″ × WOF.

Fabric: Ruby and Bliss by Bonnie and Camille for Moda

Easy HSTs

Several quilts in this book feature blocks made with half-square triangles (HSTs). These are super easy to make. Here's the method.

An HST is made with 2 contrasting squares of the same size. Place 1 square on top of the other with right sides together (Fig. A). On the back of the lighter square, draw a pencil line from one corner to the opposite corner (Fig. B). Sew ¼″ from the line on each side (Fig. C). Cut on the line to make 2 HSTs (Fig. D). Press toward the darker of the 2 fabrics. Presto!

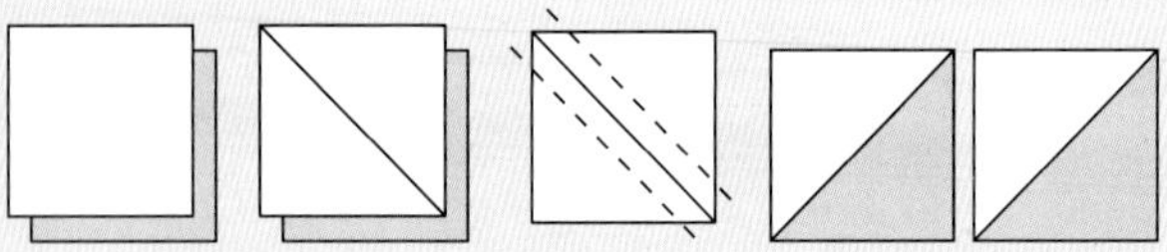

A B C D

Block Assembly

Each block is made up of 2 four-patches and 2 half-square triangles (HSTs).

1. For each four-patch, select 2 aqua squares 3½″ × 3½″ and 2 white squares 3½″ × 3½″. Following the four-patch unit assembly diagram, sew together 2 aqua/white pairs, and press the seams toward the aqua. Sew the rows together; press. Make a total of 58 aqua four-patches and 2 red ones.

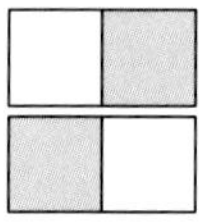

Four-patch assembly

2. To make the HSTs, refer to Easy HSTs (at left). Pair aqua and white or red and white squares 6⅞″ × 6⅞″. Make a total of 58 aqua HSTs and 2 red ones.

3. Sew 1 HST to 1 four-patch to make 1 unit as shown in the block assembly diagram. Make 2; press. Sew the 2 units together to make 1 block. Make a total of 30 blocks—29 aqua and 1 red.

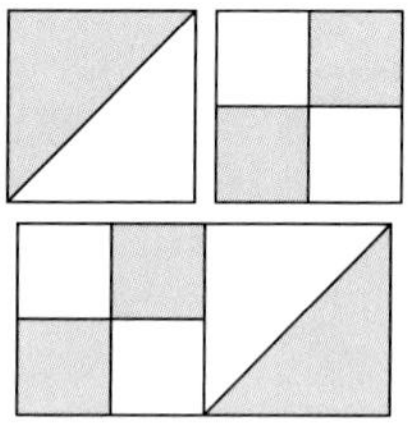

Block assembly

Quilt Assembly

1. Sew together the blocks in 6 rows of 5, with the red block in row 5, as shown in the quilt assembly diagram. Press.

2. Sew the rows together, and press.

Quilt assembly

Finishing

Photo by Camille Roskelley

1. Cut the backing fabric into 2 equal lengths (roughly 64″), and sew them together for the backing.

2. Layer the quilt top, batting, and backing, and baste to make a quilt sandwich. Machine or hand quilt as desired. Bind your quilt.

Cell Service

FINISHED QUILT: 70″ × 75″

Designer: Alissa Haight Carlton

This large lap quilt is perfect for cuddling under while on the couch. The bright colors have a strong impact and complement a room with simple, contemporary design. The big panels of fabric that make up this quilt cause it to sew up quickly and easily. Make sure you cut carefully so that the design lines up correctly.

Materials

Based on 42″ fabric width.

Fabric A (red): 2¾ yards

Fabric B (aqua): 1⅜ yards

Fabric C (ivory): 1⅜ yards for background

Backing: 4¾ yards

Binding: ⅞ yard

Please be sure to read Notes on Yardage and Piecing Large-Scale Quilts (page 56). Label the pieces as you cut.

Cutting

Fabric A (red)

1. Cut 2 strips 7½″ × WOF and sew them together end to end; trim A1.

2. Cut 2 strips 9½″ × WOF and sew them together end to end; trim A2.

3. Cut 2 strips 13½″ × WOF and sew them together end to end; trim A4.

4. Cut 1 strip 15½″ × WOF; trim A5.

5. Trim the leftover strip from Step 3 to 11½″ wide.

6. Cut 1 strip 11½″ × WOF; sew it end to end with the strip from Step 5; trim A3.

A1: 7½″ × 75½″

A2: 9½″ × 68½″

A3: 11½″ × 62½″

A4: 13½″ × 49½″

A5: 15½″ × 39½″

Fabric B (aqua)

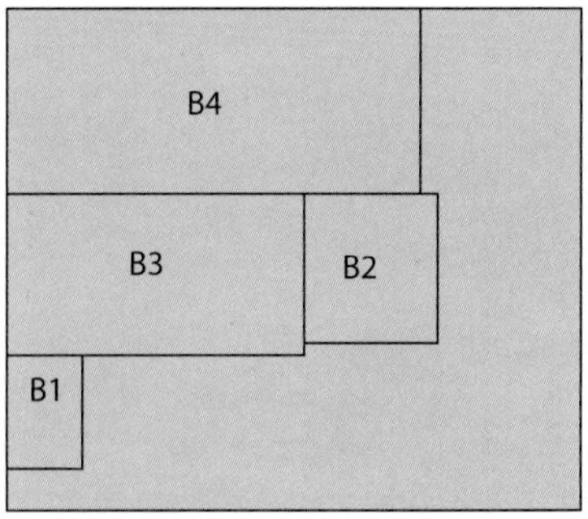

1. Cut 15½″ from the yardage parallel to the selvage; trim B4.

2. Cut 13½″ from the yardage parallel to the selvage; trim B3.

3. Cut B2.

4. Cut B1.

B1: 9½″ × 6½″

B2: 11½″ × 12½″

B3: 13½″ × 25½″

B4: 15½″ × 35½″

Fabric C (ivory)

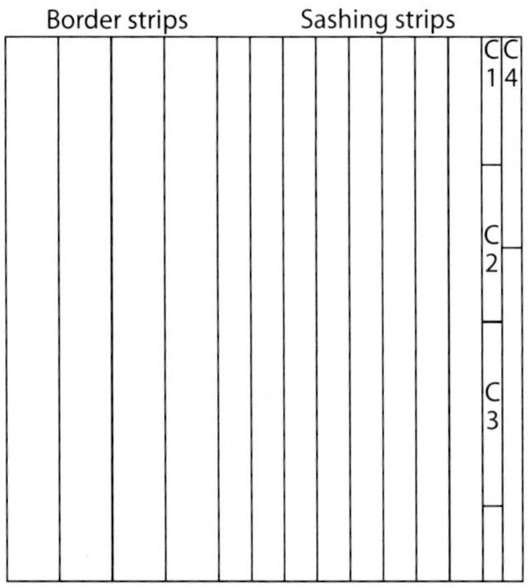

1. Cut 4 strips 4″ × WOF and sew end to end; trim to 4″ × 75½″ for the 2 border strips.

2. Cut 8 strips 2½″ × WOF and sew in pairs end to end to make 4 sashing strips. Trim to 75½″ after piecing (see Tip, below).

3. Cut 2 strips 1½″ × WOF; trim to:

   C1: 1½″ × 9½″

   C2: 1½″ × 11½″

   C3: 1½″ × 13½″

   C4: 1½″ × 15½″

TIP *In general, when piecing long strips, it's often easier for a too-long piece of fabric to be trimmed down once it has been sewn on. When cutting, think ahead and try to leave strips longer than they need to be if the pattern allows for it. Only trim them down to their perfect length after they are sewn to the pieces of fabric that surround them. This way, you are guaranteed long enough strips, rather than ones that are ¼″ too short because of small discrepancies in your piecing or cutting. We are humans and not machines—these discrepancies happen but won't cause problems if you just think ahead in this fashion. There is nothing worse than having to tear out a very long seam because you cut your piece of fabric a bit too short, when you could have just kept it extra long.*

The more you piece quilt tops, ideas such as this one will become second nature to you. These ideas are also what make quilting a more relaxing and fun process that doesn't have to be about being a fussy perfectionist.

Assembling the Quilt Top

Press after each step.

1. Sew A2, C1, and B1 into a long strip.

2. Repeat Step 1 to assemble A3, C2, B2; A4, C3, B3; and A5, C4, B4.

3. Working from left to right, assemble the quilt top.

4. Trim as necessary to square up the quilt top.

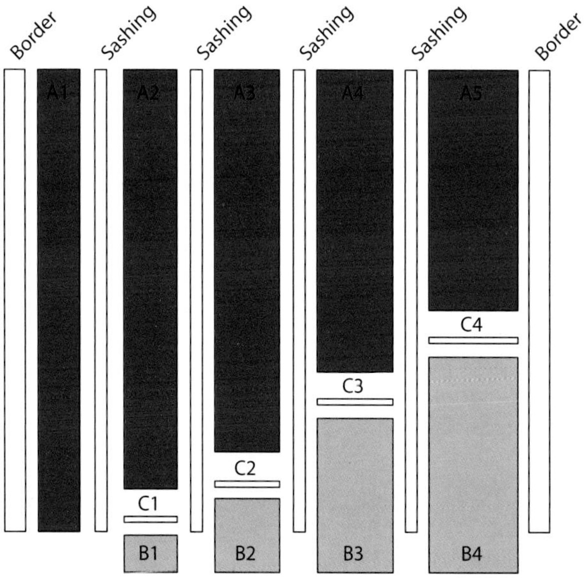

Quilt assembly

Notes on Yardage and Piecing Large-Scale Quilts

- When the measurements in a quilt pattern are longer than 42″ (the standard measurement used as the width of fabric, or WOF), you can sew together pieces of the same fabric to create one larger piece for the quilt top. This creates more seams in your quilt top, but it saves a lot of fabric and money and creates less waste. I also like the rustic and warm touch it gives these otherwise graphic designs.
- Another thing that saves yardage is not being concerned with always keeping the straight grain of the fabric going the same direction. While some quilters might disagree with this idea, it works for me. In all the quilts I have made, I have usually switched the direction of the grain of my fabric, and doing so has never caused a problem for me. The usual argument against this technique is that it changes the drape of the fabric, which is absolutely true for garment sewing. But when quilts are finished they are densely quilted, and quilting affects the drape far more than the direction in which you cut the fabric. Therefore, when it saves fabric, I switch between cutting across the grain or with the grain.
- Lastly, when quilting with solid fabrics, there is no right side or wrong side to the fabric. As a result, when putting together your quilt top, it's sometimes easy to mistakenly sew to the wrong side of the piecing. Before sewing a seam, be sure to check the already completed seams to be certain that your seam allowances are all on the same side.

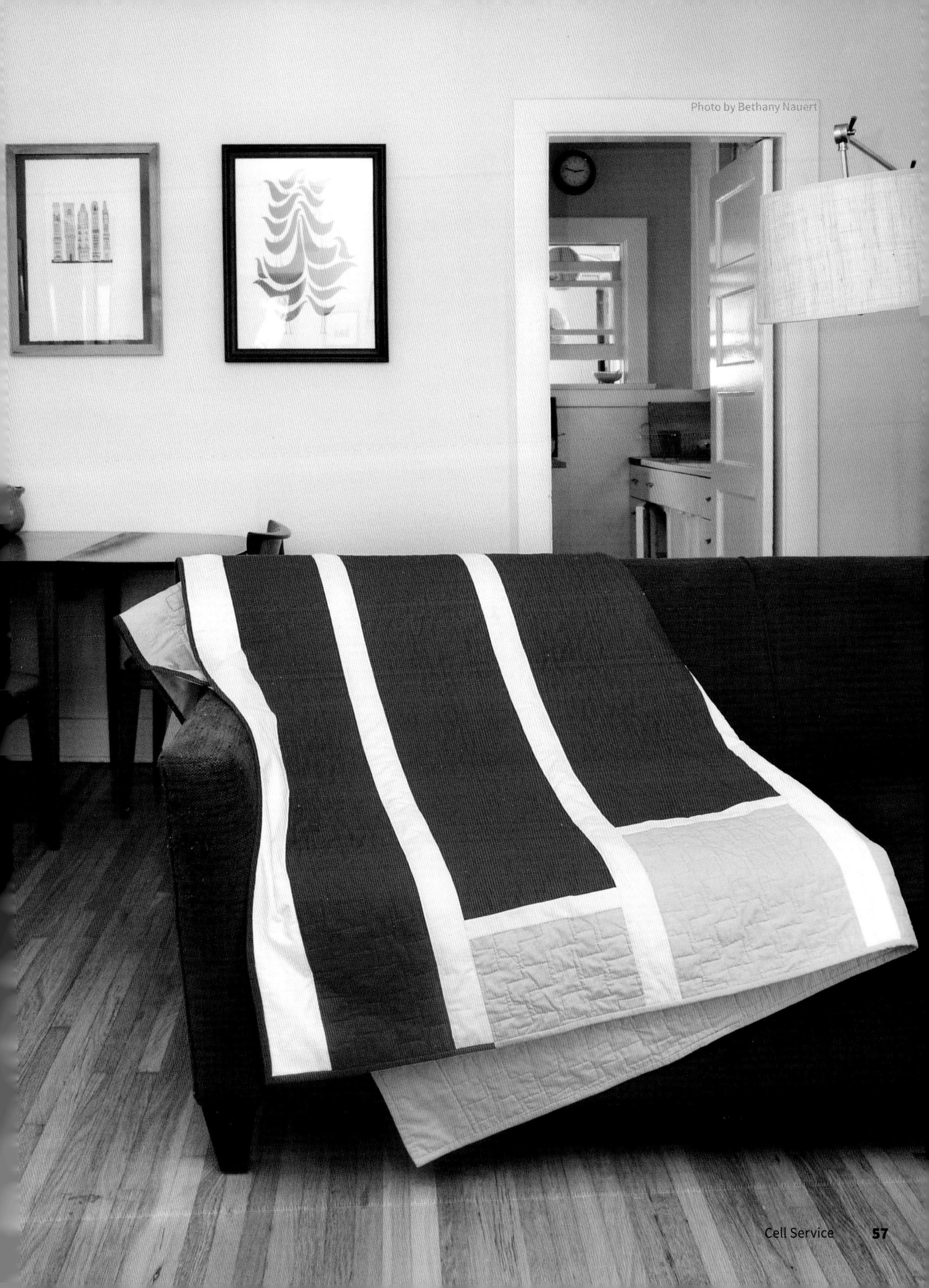
Photo by Bethany Nauert

Making the Quilt Back

To make an 80″ × 84″ quilt back, cut 2 pieces 80″ × WOF and remove the selvages. Sew the 2 pieces together along the 80″ edges.

Finishing

Layer, quilt, and bind the quilt.

If you'd like to bind this quilt as I did—with 2 colors switching and matching up with the piecing—make 93½″ of blue binding and 211½″ of red binding. Piece the 2 colors together with a straight seam. Usually I sew binding strips together with diagonal seams, but this time I wanted the look of the straight seams suddenly switching the colors.

When attaching the binding, first pin it in place. Work your way around the entire edge of the quilt, lining up the color-change seam with the quilt design. Piece together the ends, again butting them up end to end and making sure you've lined up the colors correctly.

Weaving

FINISHED QUILT: 90″ × 90″
FINISHED BLOCK: 18″ × 18″

Designers: Natalia Bonner and Kathleen Whiting
Pieced and quilted by Natalia Bonner and Kathleen Whiting

Fabric: Bella Solids by Moda Fabrics

A classic plaid design in just three colors comes to life in this cheerful quilt. The quilt appears to be set on point but it's actually put together in an easy straight setting.

Materials

Yardage is based on 42″-wide fabric.

	Baby 36″ × 36″	Throw 72″ × 72″	Coverlet 90″ × 90″
Yellow fabric	½ yard	1¼ yards	1⅞ yards
Orange fabric	1¼ yards	2¼ yards	3⅛ yards
White fabric	1¼ yards	3¼ yards	5 yards
Backing fabric	2½ yards	4½ yards	8¼ yards
Binding fabric	½ yard	⅝ yard	¾ yard
Batting	44″ × 44″	80″ × 80″	98″ × 98″

Cutting

Cut the longest strips first. Then cut the shorter strips from the leftover strips. Cut the squares diagonally twice as indicated by the symbol.

Cut		Baby 4 blocks	Throw 16 blocks	Coverlet 25 blocks
Yellow fabric	1½″ × 28″ strips	4	16	25
	1½″ × 9″ strips	16	64	100
Orange fabric	2⅝″ × 7¾″ strips	16	64	100
	2⅝″ × 11″ strips	8	32	50
White fabric	5¼″ × 5¼″ squares	16	64	100
	⊠ 8″ × 8″ squares	8 (32 triangles)	32 (128 triangles)	50 (200 triangles)

Sewing the Block

Weaving block

To make a Weaving block, follow these steps. Seam allowances are ¼″ unless otherwise indicated. Follow the pressing arrows.

1. Sew a white 5¼″ × 5¼″ square onto each side of a yellow 1½″ × 5¼″ strip. Make 2.

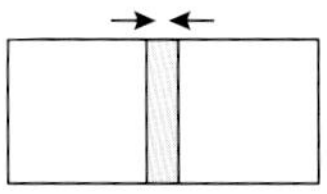

2. Sew an orange 2⅝″ × 11″ strip to the bottom of the strip set from Step 1. Make 2.

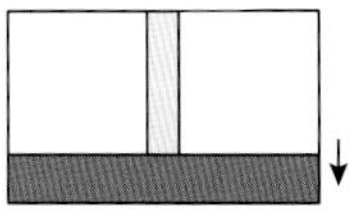

3. Sew an orange 2⅝″ × 7¾″ strip to each side of the units from Step 2 as shown. Make 2.

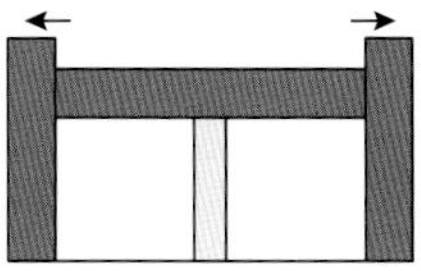

4. Sew a white triangle to the orange strips on the unit from Step 3 as shown. Then, using a ruler and rotary cutter, trim the orange strips following the angle of the triangles as shown.

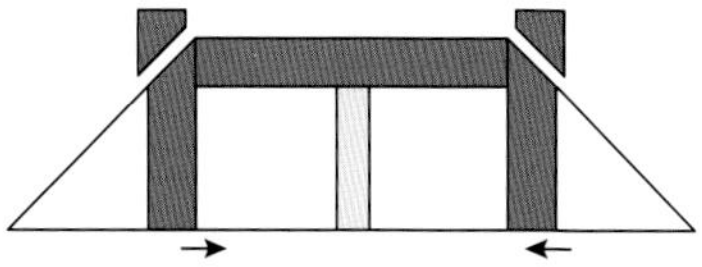

5. Sew a white triangle to each long side of the yellow 1½″ × 9″ strip. Then using a ruler and a rotary cutter, trim the end of the yellow strip, following the angles of the triangles as shown. Make 2.

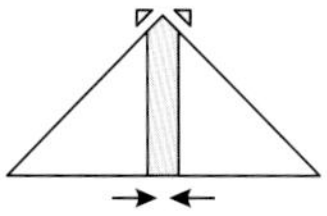

6. Sew a unit from Step 5 to a unit from Step 4. Make 2.

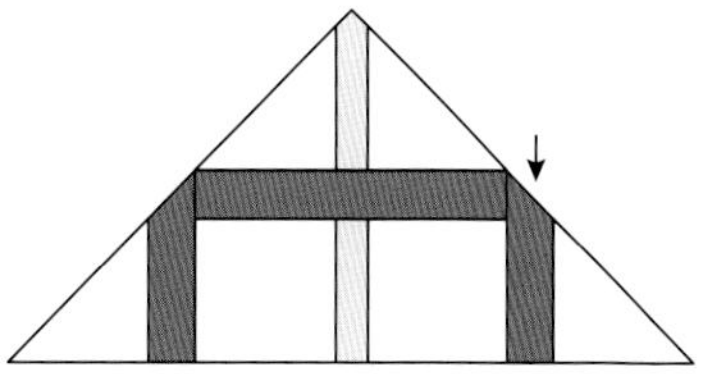

7. Match the center of the unit from Step 6 to the center of a yellow 1½″ × 28″ strip. Sew together. Then trim the ends of the yellow strip, following the angles of the white triangles as you did before.

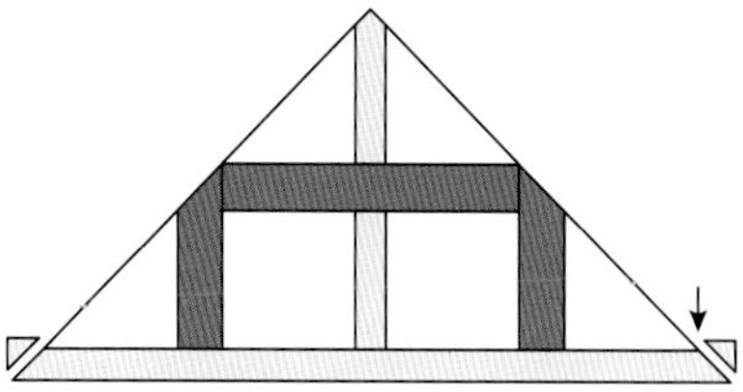

8. Referring to the Weaving block diagram, sew the remaining unit from Step 6 to the unit from Step 7 to complete the block, matching the centers and trimming the ends of the yellow strip as in Step 7.

9. Repeat these steps to make the number of blocks needed (*baby size:* 4 blocks; *throw:* 16 blocks; *coverlet:* 25 blocks).

Putting It All Together

Refer to the quilt assembly diagram to find the size quilt you are making. For the baby size, sew 2 rows of 2 blocks. For the throw, sew 4 rows of 4 blocks. For the coverlet, sew 5 rows of 5 blocks. Always press the seams in alternating directions from row to row.

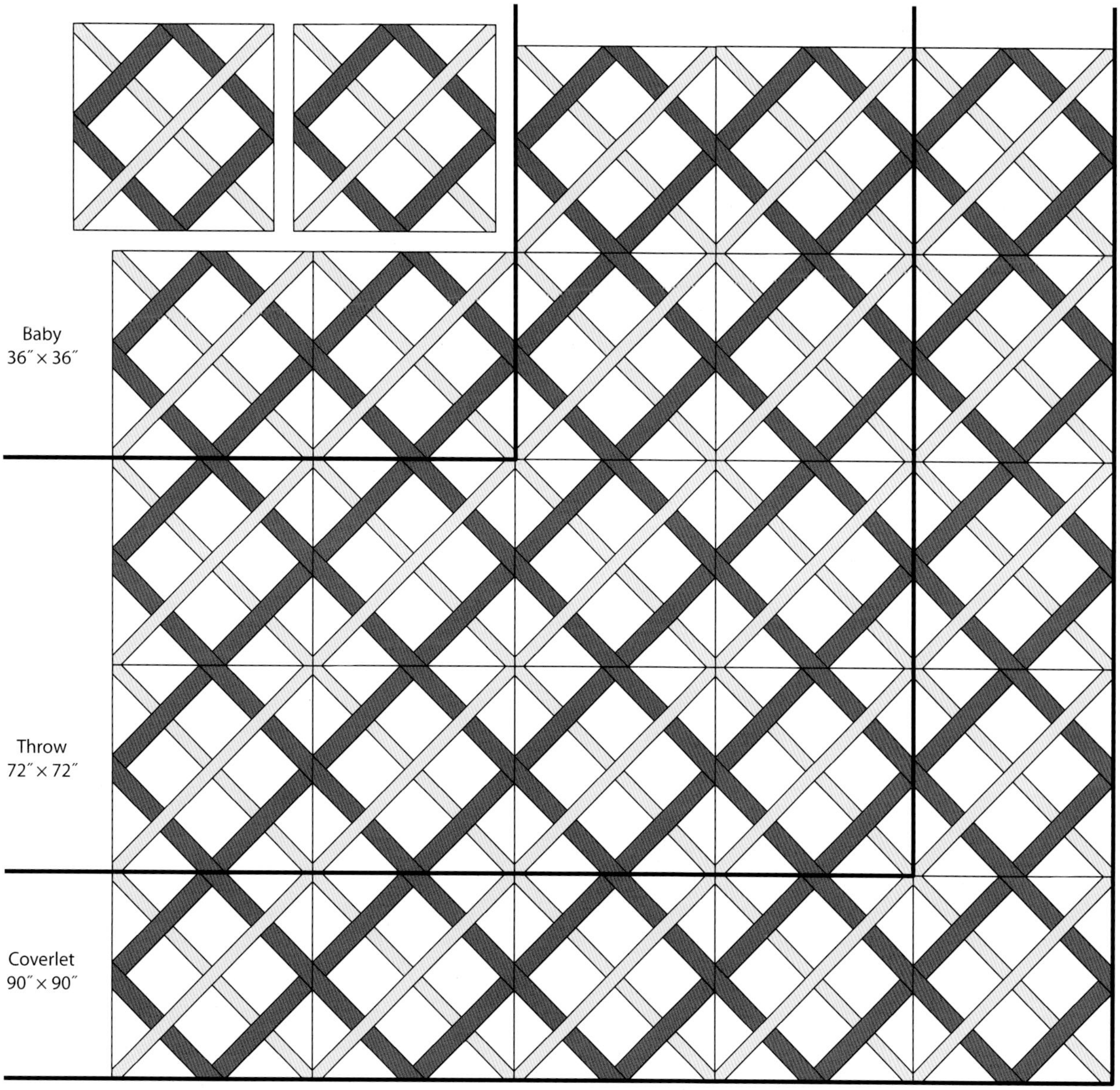

Quilt assembly

Finishing

To finish, layer, quilt, and bind the quilt as desired.

Oddballs

FINISHED QUILT: 65″ × 84″

Designer: Alissa Haight Carlton

Graphic and hip, this quilt would be loved by any recipient. A twin-size quilt, it is perfect as a large throw over a daybed or for a single bed.

Materials

Based on 42″ fabric width.

Fabric A (gray): ½ yard

Fabric B (black): 1 yard

Fabric C (blue): 6″ × 15½″

Fabric D (ivory): 5 yards

Backing: 5 yards

Binding: ⅞ yard

Please be sure to read Notes on Yardage and Piecing Large-Scale Quilts (page 56). Label the pieces as you cut.

Cutting

The color pops in the quilt are referred to as "bars." All bars are 15½″ long, but their width varies. The gray, black, and blue fabrics will be used to make the bars and are framed in background fabric before being trimmed to the correct width.

Fabric A (gray)

1. Cut 1 strip 15½″ wide.
2. Cut the strip into 3 strips:

    15½″ × 19½″

    15½″ × 9½″

    15½″ × 7″

Fabric B (black)

1. Cut 2 strips 15½″ × WOF (selvage to selvage).
2. Cut the first strip to 15½″ × 32½″.
3. Cut the second strip twice:

    15½″ × 18″

    15½″ × 14½″

Fabric C (blue)

This strip is already cut to size.

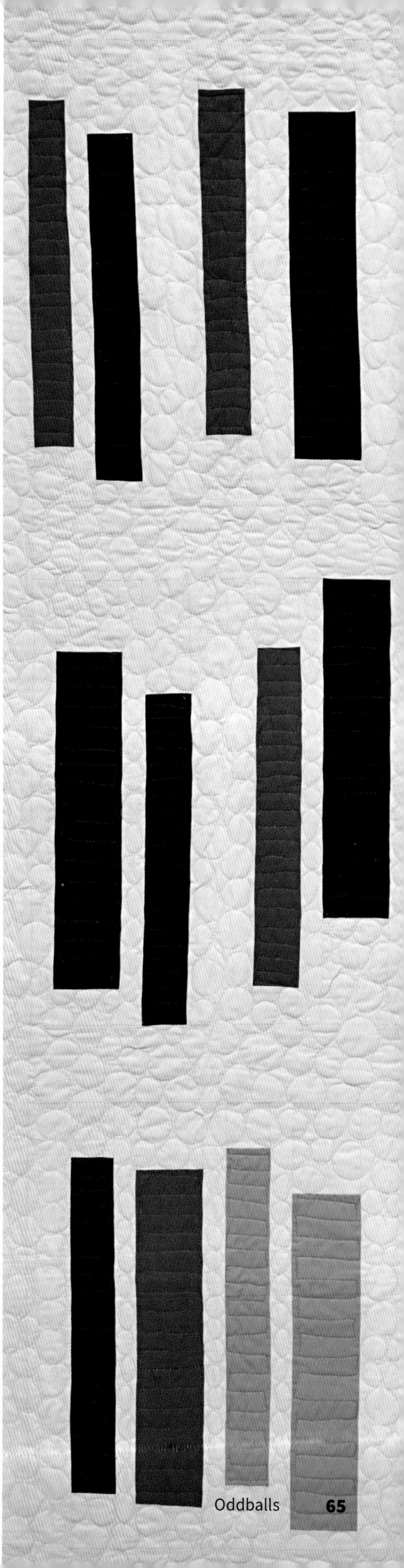

Fabric D (ivory)

Cutting out the background fabric is a bit more involved than the bars but is straightforward if you just do it step by step.

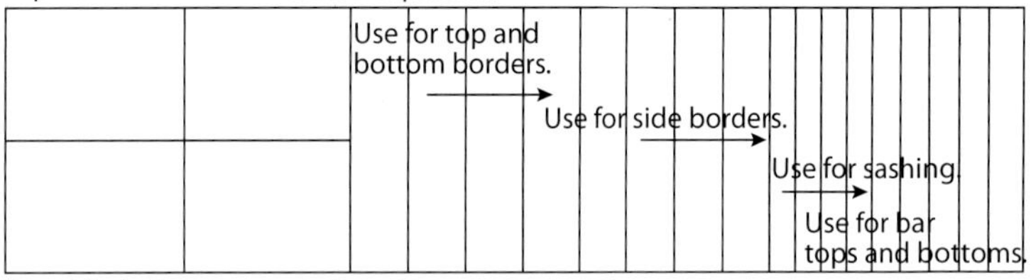

Rows 1–3 vertical strips:

1. *First cut:* Cut a piece 28″ wide × WOF. Set aside the remaining fabric.

2. *Second cut:* Cut in half, parallel to the selvages. Trim the 2 pieces 28″ wide carefully to 20½″ high.

3. Cut 1 piece (for Row 1) to:

D1: 4 strips 1½″ × 20½″

D2: 3 strips 2½″ × 20½″

D3: 4 strips 3½″ × 20½″

4. Cut the other piece (for Row 2) to:

D4: 6 strips 1½″ × 20½″

D5: 2 strips 2½″ × 20½″

D6: 4 strips 3½″ × 20½″

5. *Third cut:* Cut a piece 26″ × WOF. Set aside the remaining fabric.

6. *Fourth cut:* Trim a piece 26″ wide × 20½″ high for Row 3.

7. Cut the piece for Row 3 to:

D7: 6 strips 1½″ × 20½″

D8: 4 strips 2½″ × 20½″

D9: 2 strips 3½″ × 20½″

Bar top and bottom background:

1. Cut 6 strips 4½″ × WOF (D10).

2. Cut 1 strip 5½″ × WOF (D11).

Borders:

1. Cut 4 strips 9″ × WOF for the top and bottom borders.

2. Sew the strips in pairs end to end to make 2 long strips 9″ wide; trim each to 65½″.

3. Cut 4 strips 7½″ × WOF for the side borders.

4. Sew the strips in pairs end to end to make 2 long strips 7½″ wide; trim each to 67½″.

Sashing:

1. Cut 4 strips 4″ × WOF.

2. Sew the strips in pairs end to end to make 2 long strips 4″ wide; trim each to 51½″.

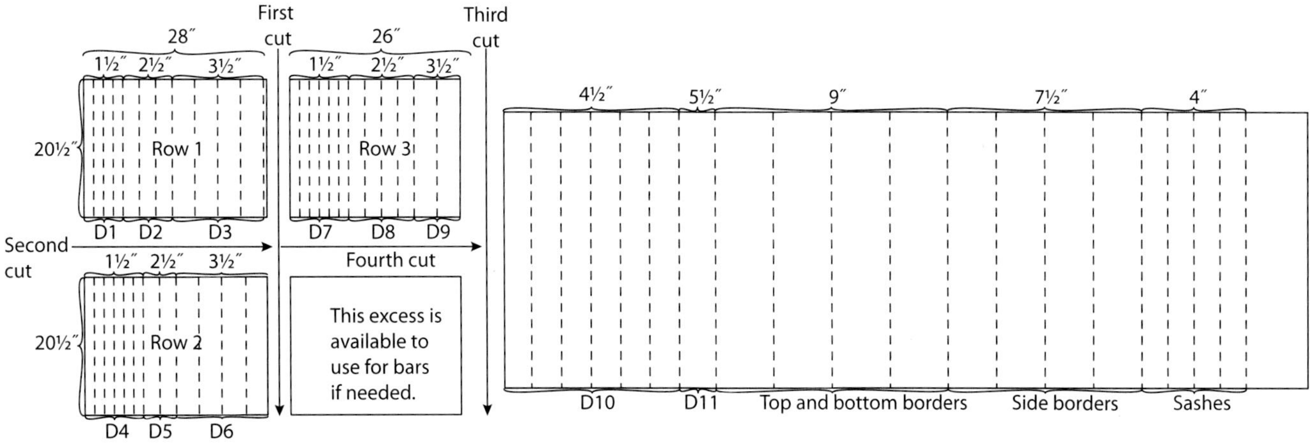

Assembling the Quilt Top

Press after each step.

Making the Bar Rows

All bars are 15″ high (finished). The "opposite sides" referred to in the following instructions could also be seen as the top and bottom.

1. Sew a D10 onto opposite sides of the 6″ × 15½″ blue bar piece; trim off the excess D10 strips. Press. Cut into the following 2 pieced components:

C1: 2½″ wide

C2: 3½″ wide

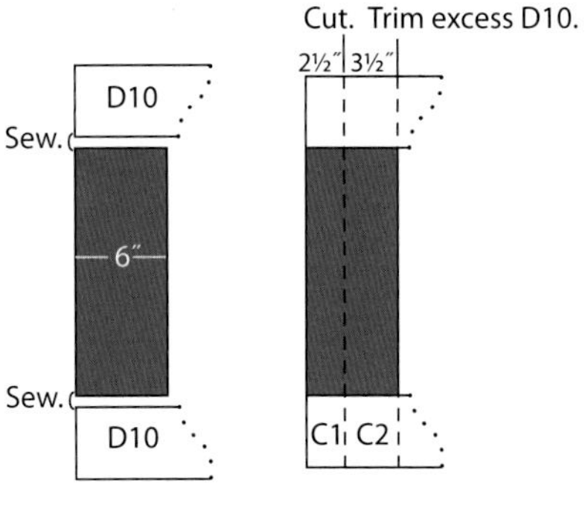

2. Sew a D10 onto opposite sides of the 32½″ × 15½″ black bar piece; trim off the excess D10 strips. Press. Cut into the following 11 pieced components:

B1: 2½″ wide

B2: 3½″ wide

B3: 2½″ wide

B5: 3½″ wide

B6: 3½″ wide

B8: 3½″ wide

B11: 3½″ wide

B12: 2½″ wide

B13: 2½″ wide

B14: 1½″ wide

B15: 3½″ wide

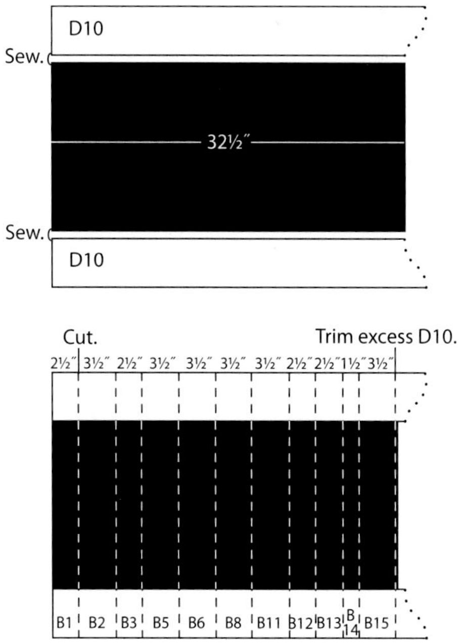

3. Sew a D10 onto opposite sides of the 18″ × 15½″ black bar piece. Trim off the excess D10 strips. Press. Cut the following 6 pieced components:

B16: 2½″ wide

B17: 3½″ wide

B18: 2½″ wide

B19: 3½″ wide

B20: 2½″ wide

B22: 3½″ wide

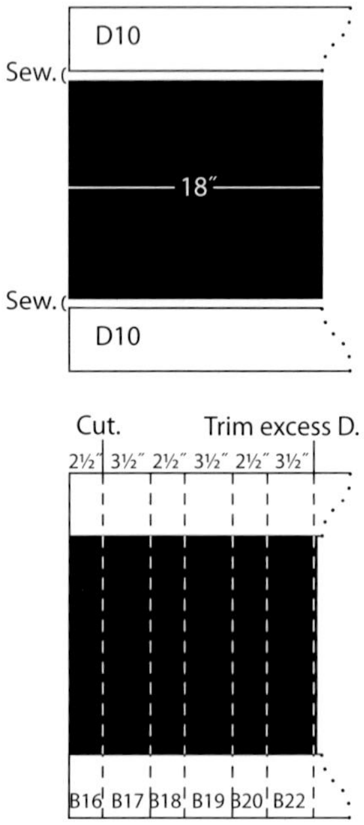

4. Sew a D10 onto opposite sides of the 19½″ × 15½″ gray bar piece. Trim off the excess D10 strips. Press. Cut the following 7 pieced components:

A1: 2½″ wide

A2: 2½″ wide

A3: 2½″ wide

A4: 2½″ wide

A5: 3½″ wide

A6: 2½″ wide

A8: 3½″ wide

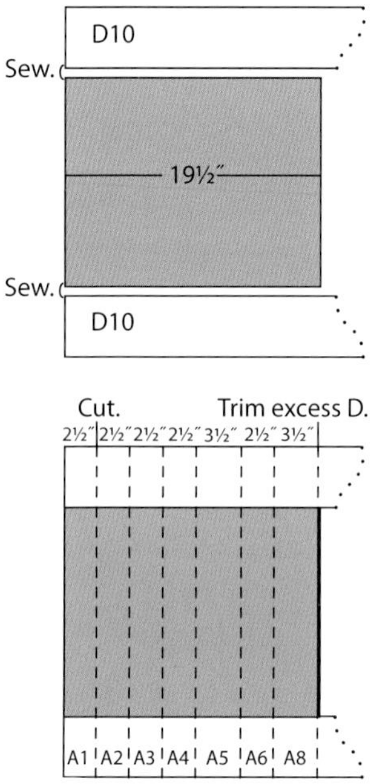

5. Sew a D10 onto opposite sides of the 7″ × 15½″ gray bar piece. Trim off the excess D10 strips. Press. Cut the following 2 pieced components:

A9: 3½″ × 15½″

A10: 3½″ × 15½″

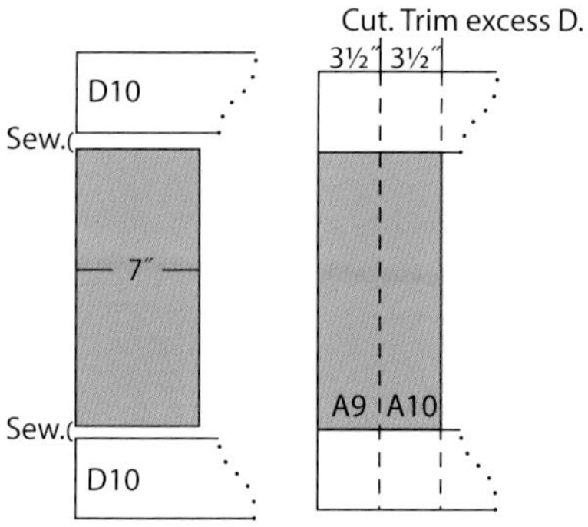

6. Sew a D11 onto only one side of the remaining gray bar piece. Trim off the excess D11 strip. Press. Cut the following 3 pieced components:

A7: 2½″ × 15½″

A11: 3½″ × 15½″

A12: 3½″ × 15½″

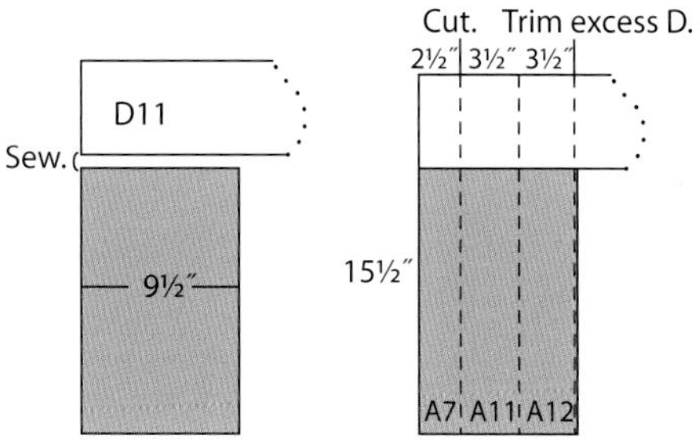

7. Sew a D11 onto only one side of the remaining black bar piece. Trim off the excess D11 strip. Press. Cut the following 5 pieced components:

B4: 3½″ wide

B7: 2½″ wide

B9: 2½″ wide

B10: 3½″ wide

B21: 2½″ wide

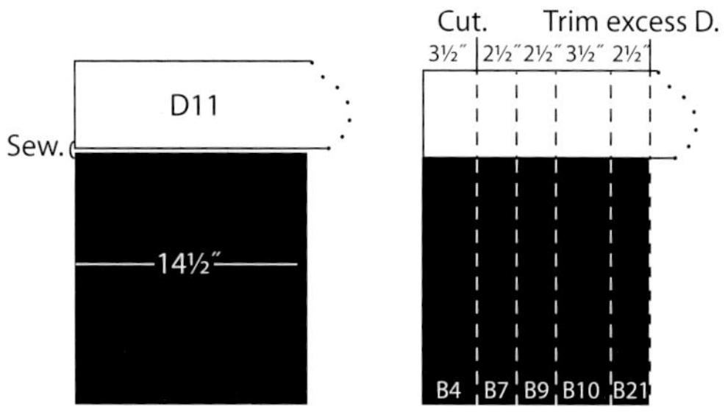

8. Working with bars A1, A5, B12, B16, and B20, trim the white background ends on both ends to 2¾″. Each bar will measure 20½″ long.

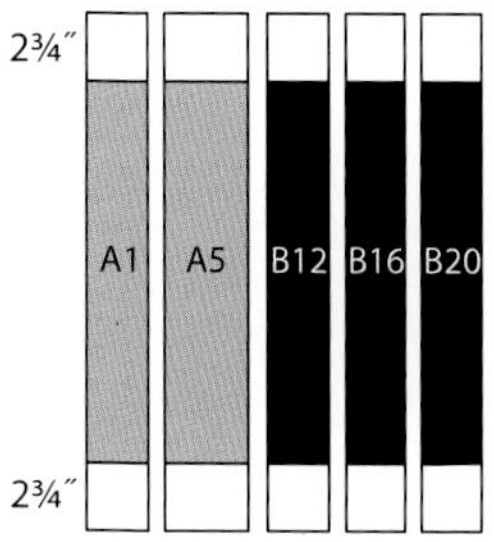

9. Working with A2, A4, A6, A8, B2, B5, B8, B11, B14, B22, and C1, trim the white background on the top end to 2¼″ and trim the white background on the bottom end to 3¼″. When you place the bars into their respective rows, turn bars A6, B2, B8, B11, and B14 upside down. Each bar will measure 20½″ long.

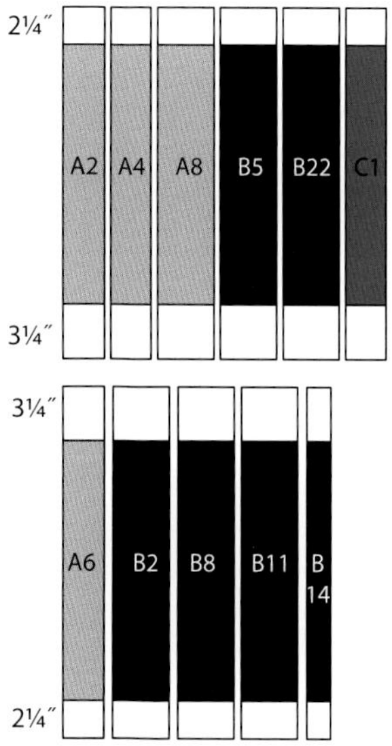

10. Working with A3, B1, B3, B6, B13, B15, B17, B18, B19, and C2, trim the white background on the top end to 1¼″. When you place the bars into their respective rows, turn bars B1, B6, B13, B17, B19, and C2 upside down. Each bar will measure 20½″ long.

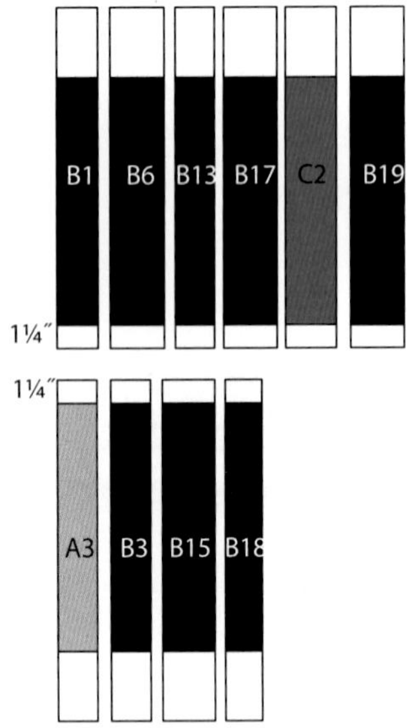

11. Next, working row by row and from left to right, use the bars and the Fabric D background strips and piece together Rows 1, 2, and 3. Press. It is important to keep a uniform seam allowance during this process so that the rows all end up the same length. Carefully reference the assembly diagram (below) to make sure that you're piecing everything in the correct order and using the correct widths of background fabric between the bars.

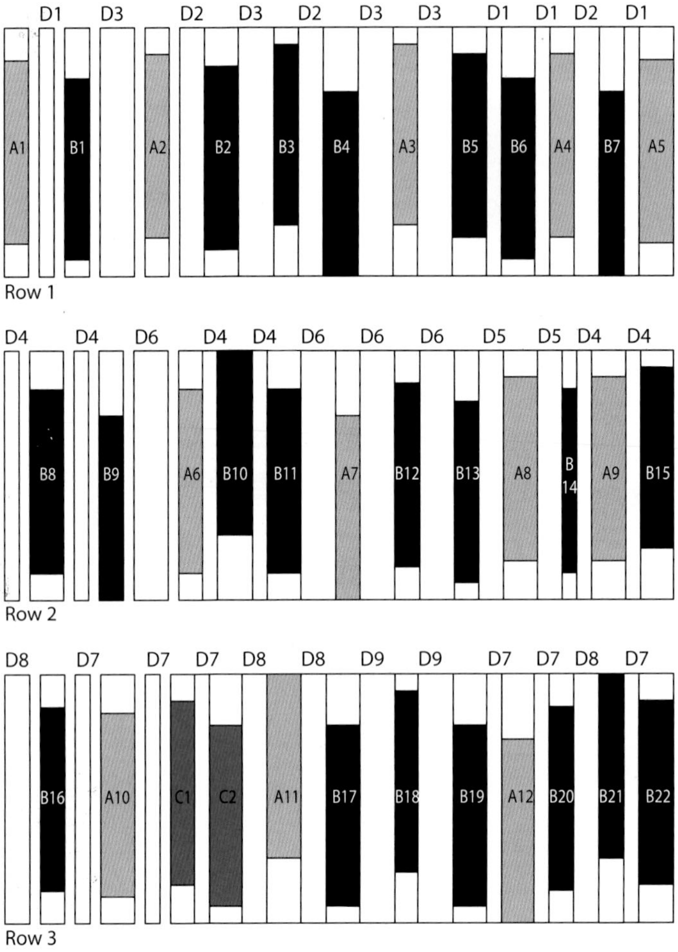

Quilt assembly

Adding Sashing and Borders

1. Sew the 3 rows to the 2 sashing strips and press.
2. Add the side borders and press.
3. Add the top and bottom borders and press.

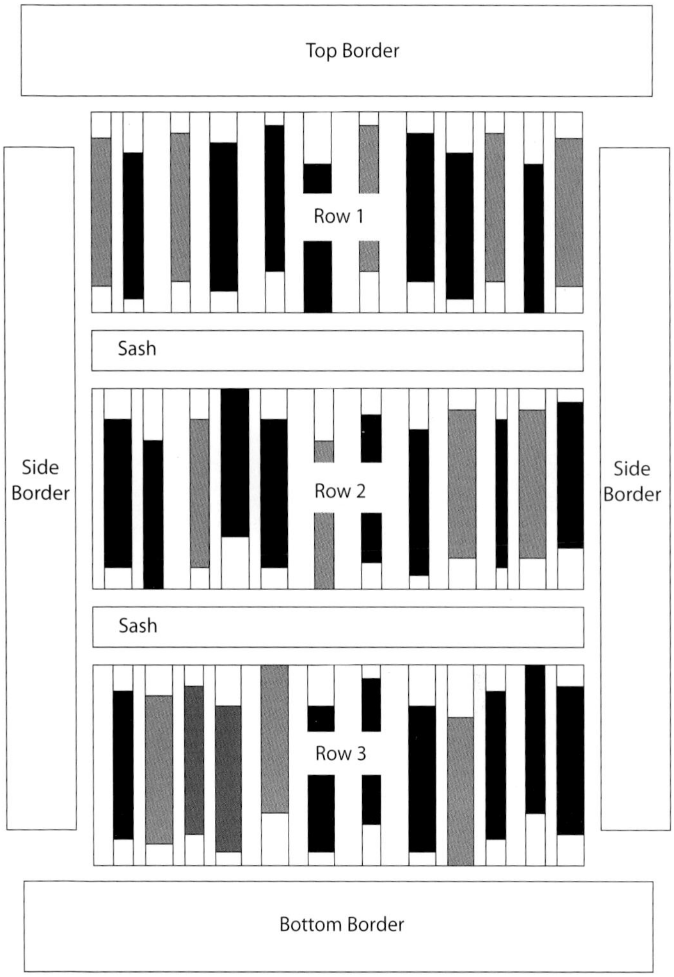

Making the Quilt Back

To make a 75″ × 94″ quilt back, cut 2 pieces 75″ × WOF and remove the selvages. Sew the 2 pieces together along the 75″ edges. Then add 10″ more to the bottom as follows: Cut 2 strips 10½″ × WOF, piece them together end to end, trim to 75″, and sew the long strip to the bottom of the quilt back.

Quilting

Quilt as desired.

One option: I created a lot of texture on this quilt by doing two different types of free-motion quilting. First, I stitched a straight-line rectangular pattern to fill in all the bars. Then, I worked my way around the quilt top, filling in all the open space with pebble quilting.

Patterns

Daisy Drop

(page 13)

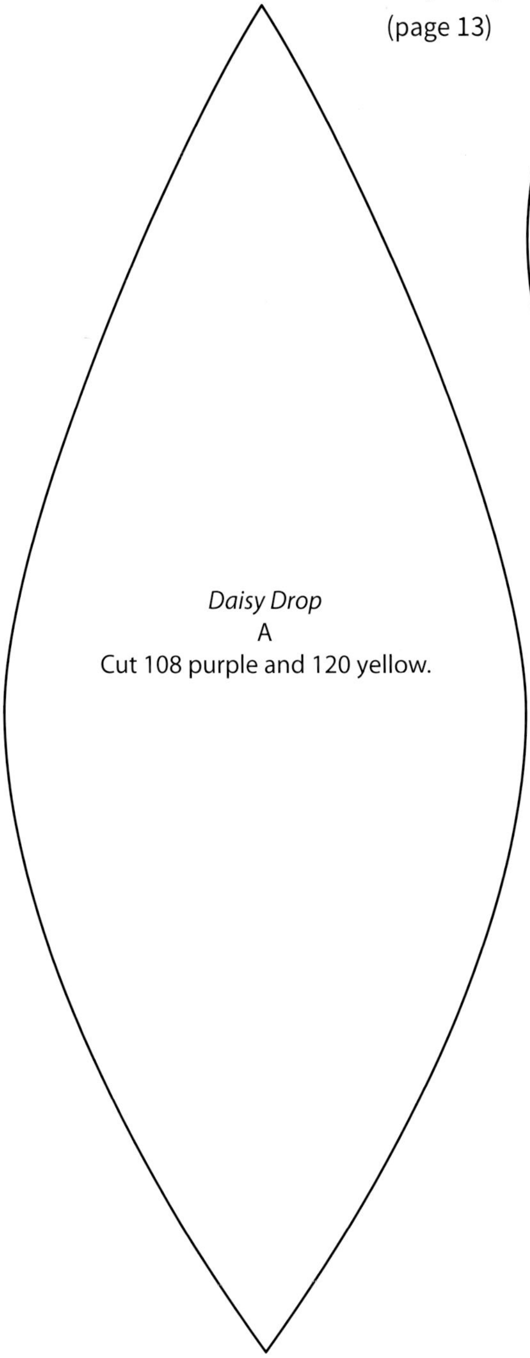

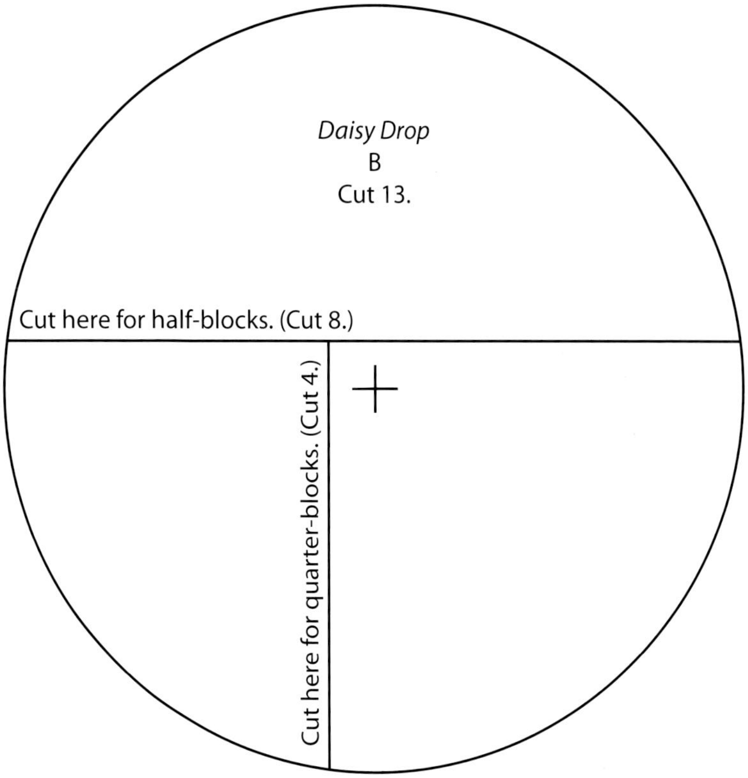

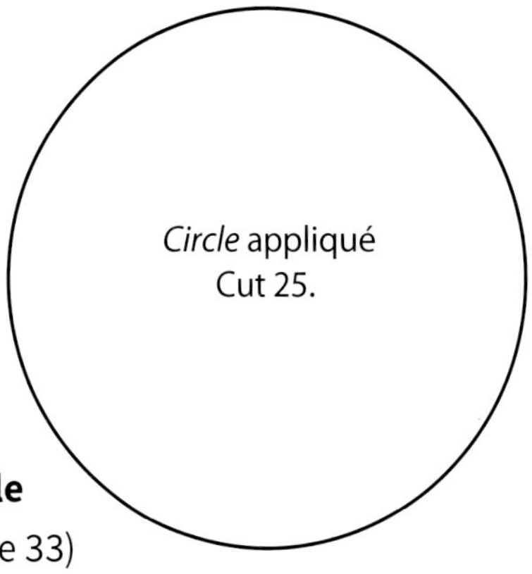

Circle

(page 33)

Flowered Dishes

(page 21)

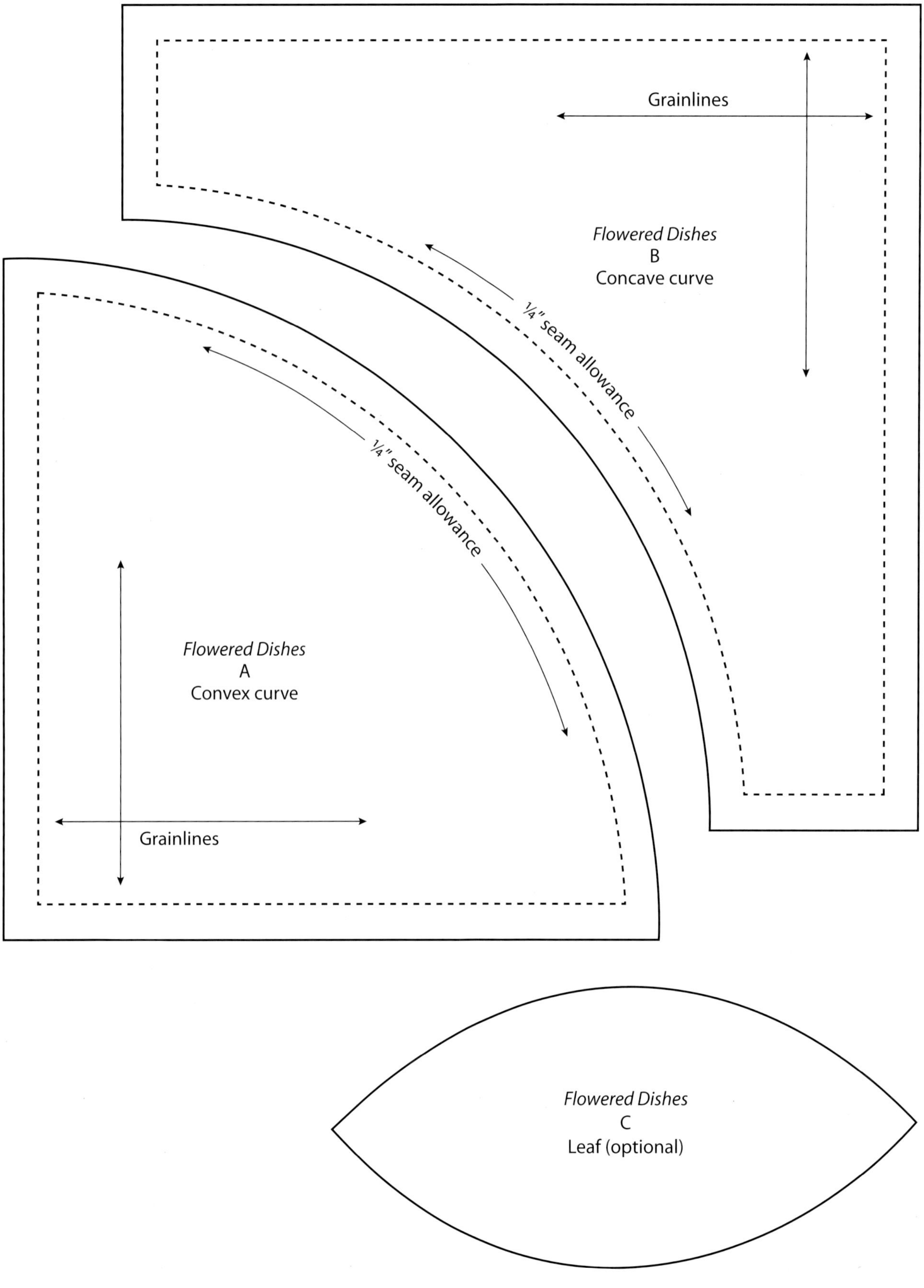

About the Designers

Photo by Stephen Whiteside

ALETHEA BALLARD fell in love with sewing at the age of ten and has been making quilts ever since. Her "maverick" style combines her impatience with convention, her spontaneity, and her artistic sensibility. Alethea lives in the San Francisco Bay Area. • **maverickquilts.wordpress.com**

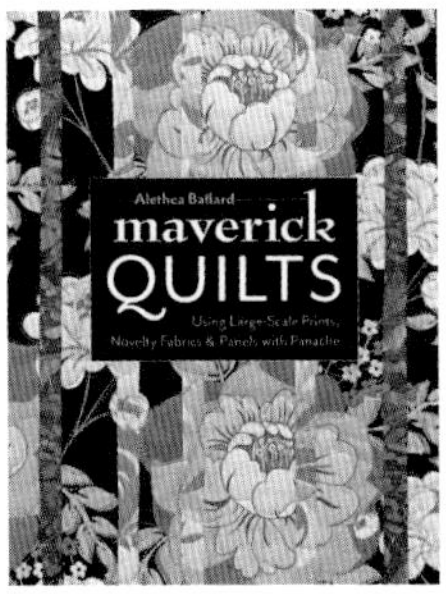

Flowered Dishes (page 21) originally appeared in *Maverick Quilts* by Alethea Ballard, available from C&T Publishing.

Photos by Whitnee North

NATALIA BONNER has been quilting professionally for many years. She is a teacher, pattern designer, and popular blogger with numerous awards for her work. Natalia lives in St. George, Utah. • **piecenquilt.com**

KATHLEEN WHITING has been sewing for decades. In 2010 she was named the first *McCall's Quilting* Quilt Design Star. She has won numerous awards for her quilts, and her designs have been published in several magazines. Kathleen lives in Heber, Utah.

Daisy Drop (page 13) originally appeared in *Beginner's Guide to Free-Motion Quilting* by Natalia Bonner; *Weaving* (page 59) originally appeared in *Modern One-Block Quilts* by Natalia Bonner and Kathleen Whiting; available from Stash Books.

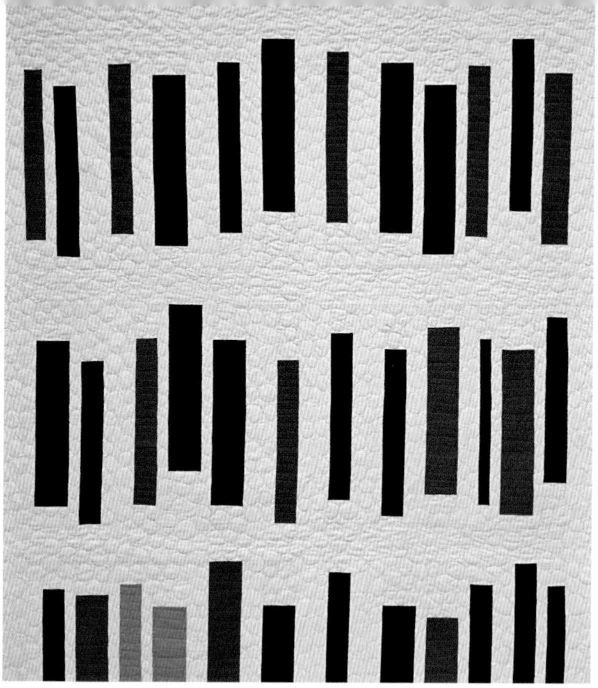

ALISSA HAIGHT CARLTON is one of the founders of the Modern Quilt Guild. Her work has been published in *Stitch* magazine, *Quilter's Home*, and Quilting Arts' *Quilt Scene*. When not quilting, she casts reality stars for television shows. Alissa lives in Los Angeles.

alissahaightcarlton.com

Photo by Ashlee House

CHERRI HOUSE is a quilt designer and co-owner of Cherry House Quilts. Geometric and graphic quilts designed as a whole are Cherri's signature style. Cherri believes that people in her home will always feel welcome when they are "warm with a quilt." Cherri lives in Humble, Texas.

Cell Service (page 53) and *Oddballs* (page 64) originally appeared in *Modern Minimal* by Alissa Haight Carlton, available from Stash Books.

City Lights (page 28) originally appeared in *City Quilts* by Cherri House, available from Stash Books.

AMANDA MURPHY worked as a graphic designer and art director before she discovered quilting. She markets quilt patterns under the Amanda Murphy Designs label, and is a C&T author, a fabric designer, a Craftsy teacher, and a BERNINA quilting and longarm spokesperson. She lives in North Carolina.

amandamurphydesign.com

Crossroads (page 7) originally appeared in *Modern Holiday* by Amanda Murphy, available from Stash Books.

CAMILLE ROSKELLEY Growing up in a home brimming with creativity and quilts, Camille became a talented quilter and designer. She's now a fabric designer for Moda, a book author, a Craftsy quilting teacher, and a quilt pattern designer for her own company, Thimble Blossoms. Camille lives in Las Vegas, Nevada.

camilleroskelley.com

Retro (page 48) originally appeared in *Simply Retro with Camille Roskelley*, available from Stash Books.

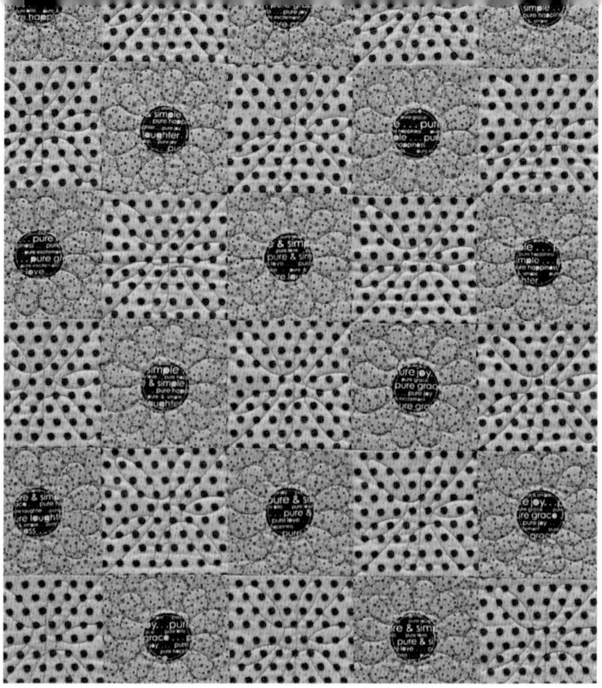

KIM SCHAEFER is a best-selling author and the founder of Little Quilt Company, which is known for its small, fun-to-make quilting patterns. A fabric designer with Andover Fabrics, Kim lives in Southeastern Wisconsin. • **littlequiltcompany.com**

SWEETWATER was founded in 2001 by Karla Eisenach and her two daughters, Lisa Burnett and Susan Kendrick. Located in Colorado, Sweetwater's simple yet sophisticated aesthetic infuses their many product lines, including fabric and quilt patterns for Moda.
thesweetwaterco.com

Interweave (page 18) originally appeared in *Bright & Bold Cozy Modern Quilts* by Kim Schaefer, available from C&T Publishing.

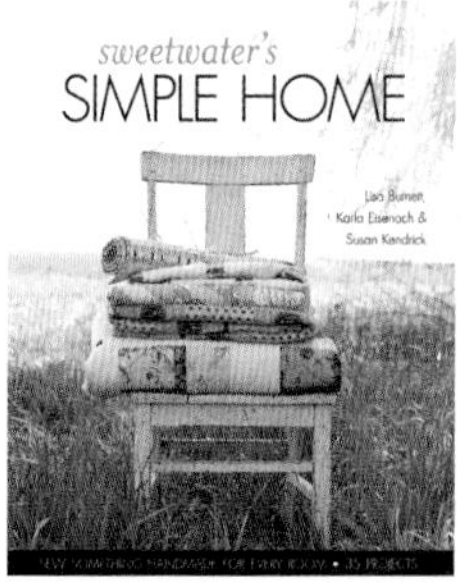

Circle (page 33) originally appeared in *Sweetwater's Simple Home* by Karla Eisenach, Lisa Burnett, and Susan Kendrick, available from Stash Books.

AMY WALSH has a lifelong passion for sewing, quilting, and fabric. In 2004, she left her job teaching history and started working as a longarm quilter. She started Blue Underground Studios, Inc., with fellow longarm quilter Janine Burke in 2005. Amy lives in Chicago. • **blueundergroundstudios.com**

ANGELA WALTERS is a machine quilter who loves to teach others to use quilting to bring out the best in their quilt tops. Her work has been published in numerous magazines and books. She shares tips and finished quilts on her blog and believes that "quilting is the funnest part!" Angela lives in Kansas City, Missouri. • **quiltingismytherapy.com**

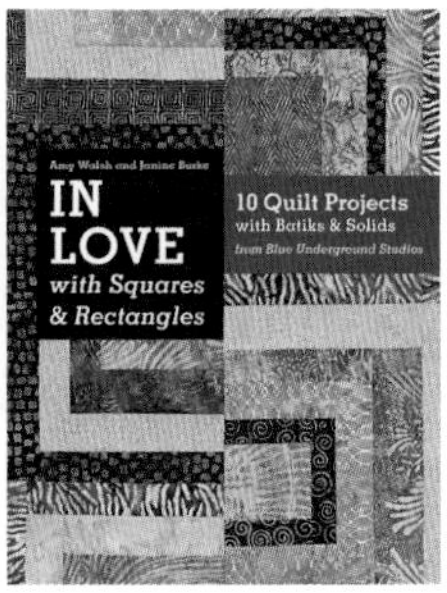

Lake Shore Drive (page 38) originally appeared in *Colorful Quilts for Fabric Lovers* by Amy Walsh and Janine Burke; *All the Above* (page 43) originally appeared in *In Love with Squares & Rectangles* by Amy Walsh and Janine Burke; available from C&T Publishing.

Basket Case (page 4) originally appeared in *In the Studio with Angela Walters*, available from Stash Books.

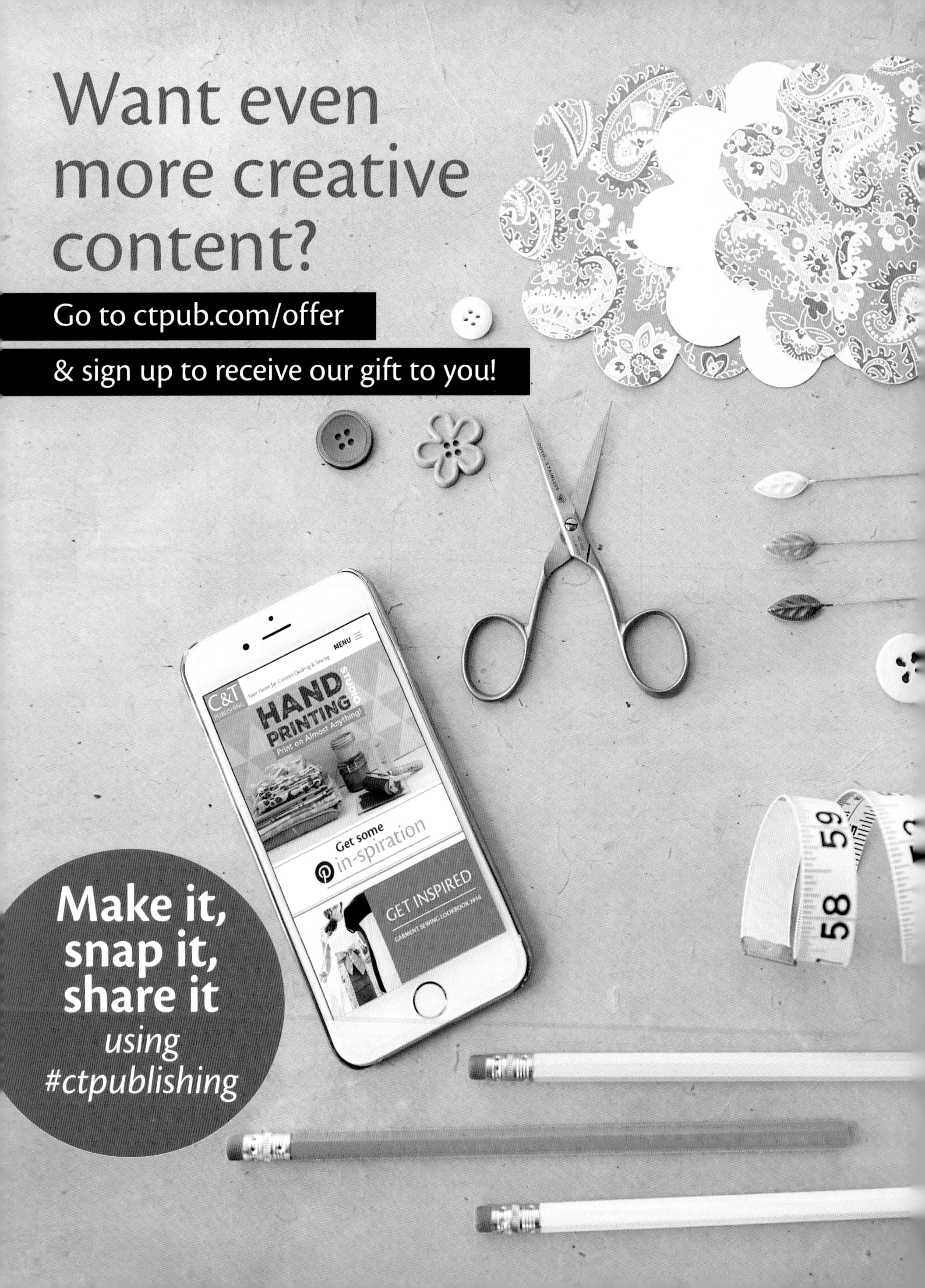

Want even more creative content?
Go to ctpub.com/offer
& sign up to receive our gift to you!
MENU
C&T PUBLISHING
Your Home for Creative Quilting & Sewing
HAND PRINTING STUDIO
Print on Almost Anything!
Get some in-spiration
GET INSPIRED
GARMENT SEWING LOOKBOOK 2016
Make it, snap it, share it
using #ctpublishing